ALSO BY T. RAPHAEL SIMONS

Feng Shui Step by Step

Feng Shui Strategies for Business Success

the FENG SHUI of love

Arranging Your Home to Attract and Hold Love—
with Personalized Astrological Charts and Forecasts

T. RAPHAEL SIMONS

GRAMERCY BOOKS
NEW YORK

This 2007 edition is published by Gramercy Books,
an imprint of Random House Value Publishing, by arrangement
with Three Rivers Press, divisions of Random House, Inc., New York.

Gramercy is a registered trademark and the colophon is a trademark of Random House, Inc.

Random House
New York • Toronto • London • Sydney • Auckland
www.randomhouse.com

Printed and bound in the United States of America.

Design by Jan Derevjanik

A catalog record for this title is available from the Library of Congress.

ISBN: 978-0-517-22854-8

10 9 8 7 6 5 4 3 2 1

To Ellen Simons

Acknowledgments

To Chieh Lin, Shuang Hsien, Han Shan, and Shih Te, who were the inspirations for this book, I owe my gratitude. I also wish to express my sincere thanks to Zeng Xianwen for his beautiful calligraphy; to Terry Lee, without whose instruction I would never have learned this wondrous art of feng shui; to Sue Herner, my agent, for her perpetual encouragement and friendship; to Annetta Hanna, my editor, whose insights gave wings to the writing of this book; to my amazing copyeditor, Susan Brown; to John Son, my assistant editor, for his ready help; to Camille Smith, Marysarah Quinn, and everyone else at Three Rivers Press who helped to bring this book to fruition; to my students, Jackie Albert, Celia Berliner, Anita Fischer, and Marilyn Toole, who patiently put up with me while cheering me on these past few months; and, finally, to you, dear reader, who in implementing the ideas in this book, will be magnifying the spirit of love.

contents

How to Use This Book

The Feng Shui of Love is written as a guide to help you create a personally meaningful home environment that attracts and keeps love in your life. As do my previous books, it contains personalized astrological material that not only reveals many interesting things about you and your relationships but also indicates the best directions in space and colors for you to use to attract love. *The Feng Shui of Love*, however, is based on an astrological method quite different from that of my previous books.

There are two Chinese astrological systems used traditionally in feng shui. Their names are Jyo Hsing, or Nine Star, and Ba Tzu, or Four Pillars. Because they fit together like a hand in a glove, these two systems, with their analogous compass methods, can be used in tandem. They also can be used separately. This book is based on the Four Pillars method, famous for its twelve zodiac signs—Rat, Ox, Tiger, Rabbit, Dragon, Snake, Horse, Sheep, Monkey, Rooster, Dog, and Pig. I have chosen this method because it yields a special astrological significator called the relationship element. Your relationship element, as you'll soon discover, provides you with a uniquely effective key for arranging your home around the theme of romantic love that no other astrological method has to offer.

Over the past few years, since the publication of my first book, I have received letters from people living in Australia, New Zealand, and South Africa asking whether the compass directions of the Chinese elements are different for the Southern Hemisphere than for the Northern Hemisphere. The answer is no.

1

The astrological and compass coordinates in the Chinese system are the same for the whole planet. The element Water corresponds to the north magnetic pole, and the element Fire corresponds to the south magnetic pole. Thus, the compass directions and colors as given in this book are universally applicable. For a complete discussion of this interesting question, please visit my Web site: www.TRS-fengshui.com.

The supplies you will need to use this book are a few photocopies of the floor plan of your home and a compass, which you can find in most hardware, Army-Navy, or sporting goods stores. You will find precise instructions on how to work with your floor plan and compass in the preface to Part Two (How to Use Part Two).

As you proceed through Part One, you will be filling out questionnaires, consulting Chinese astrological charts for your date of birth, and listing all the data specific to you. You will find the charts easy to use and your personal data effective in arranging your home. You may list your personal data either on the form provided here or on a separate sheet of paper.

To enjoy the full benefit of this book, please read it chapter by chapter. Its material is built in a logical, step-by-step fashion. Upon understanding it, you will be able to use it in a truly effective way. This method of feng shui works. I wish you the best of luck in using it.

Personal Data

1. Your yin or yang style of relating _____

2. Your favored element _____

3. What your favored element means for the arrangement of your home

    _____

    _____

4. Your personal element (element of your day of birth) and its

    corresponding colors _____

    _____

5. Your partner's personal element and its corresponding colors _____

    _____

6. Your relationship element and its corresponding direction or directions in

    space and colors _____

    _____

7. Your partner's relationship element and its corresponding direction or

    directions in space and colors _____

    _____

8. Your element or elements of mutual harmony and their corresponding

    direction or directions in space and colors _____

    _____

9. Your area of special interest _____

10. What your area of special interest means for the arrangement of your

    home _____

    _____

11. Corresponding colors and directions in space for your area of special

    interest _____

12. Your partner's area of special interest _____

13. What your partner's area of special interest means for the arrangement of

    your home _____

    _____

14. Corresponding colors and directions in space for your partner's area of

    special interest _____

15. Environmental suggestions corresponding to the signs of your year and

    day of birth _____

16. Environmental suggestions corresponding to the signs of your partner's

    year and day of birth _____

part one

Discovering Your Personal Style

chapter 1

Your Heart, Your Home, and Your Relationships

Feng shui is an ancient Taoist art. According to Taoist philosophy, everything that exists is a disclosure of the Tao. The Tao is boundless Unity.

Inherent in the Tao is a set of first principles, or elements, which give rise to all phenomena in nature. These five elements are Water, Wood, Fire, Earth, and Metal. The five elements, as concepts, form the theoretical basis of all Taoist arts, including Chinese astrology, feng shui, classical Chinese music, Chinese medicine, chi kung, Chinese cooking, painting, calligraphy, and so forth.

Feng shui may be described as the art of arranging space in order to bring about desired changes in one's life and circumstances. It is based on a profound knowledge of the ways environmental and mental conditions affect one another.

According to Taoist philosophy, there is no real division between your mind and environment. Because they are both disclosures of the Tao, your mind and environment constitute an organic continuum. The relation between your mind and environment can be viewed in two ways:

- Your actions, stemming from your positive and negative mental states, affect the condition of your environment.
- Your environment is everything that attracts your attention; it affects your mental states and resultant actions.

In the simplest of terms, outer causes affect inner conditions, and inner causes affect outer conditions. Inner and outer causes and conditions always behave cyclically. Their effects are reciprocal. In other words, what you do to your environment, you do to yourself.

In terms of feng shui, this inner-outer relation implies two equally meaningful approaches to the practice. Let's look at each of them in turn.

How Mental States Affect Environmental Conditions

Your state of mind is fundamentally an energetic state. Happiness, sorrow, anger, peacefulness, and love are qualities of energy, or vibrations, that we automatically convey to our surroundings. Have you ever gone to someone's home and felt particularly happy there, even though the place seemed ordinary? Or have you ever gone to someone's home that was arranged beautifully but felt lifeless, or even disturbed? A home always reflects the prevailing mood, or energetic state, of its occupants. If you are creative and imaginative at heart, your home will reflect your joy. But, if you are often depressed and angry, your home will reflect your stress, no matter how nicely you arrange it.

Because the vibrations of your home reflect your moods or energetic states, you can modify its vibrations by consciously modifying your inner state. This means that if you want your home to attract and hold love, begin by cultivating peace and harmony in yourself. If you set these conditions inwardly, eventually they will manifest outwardly.

The ancient Chinese believed that the collective condition of the people affected the weather patterns and productivity of the land. The sages taught that being at one with the Tao would allow heaven and earth to interact freely so that nature would freely and simply produce its changes and give the people what they wanted. As Lao Tzu put it:

> The Tao does nothing, yet there is nothing it does not do.
> If kings and princes were able to dwell in it,
> All things would be transformed by themselves.

If they desired to control the process of transformation
I would restrain them by the nameless simplicity.
Nameless simplicity is free of aims.
Free of aims, it is at peace.
The world will find peace by itself.

In the context of the Tao, love is a peaceful interaction of the forces of nature. Following this, you should begin the transformation of your home by generating peaceful conditions in yourself. Cultivate loving-kindness, joy, and compassion. In addition, treat yourself as much as possible to things that evoke your romantic feelings, such as fine clothes, fine foods, beautiful music, and so forth. Cultivate all that appeals to your personal sense of beauty. Generate feelings of ease and inner harmony. Relax, and let go of your worries.

One of the most important keys to generating peaceful conditions in life is to establish healthy boundaries. Establishing healthy boundaries depends to a great extent upon cultivating self-respect and self-esteem.

If you've been disappointed by love in the past, let it go and let it be. Cultivate good friendships with people who share your views and are supportive. Keep those who distress you at a polite distance. Have confidence in yourself.

Your state of inner harmony will greatly influence the decisions you make as you carry out the process of this book. If you maintain joyful and confident feelings while arranging the feng shui of your home, your home will be filled with the most wonderful energy, which will attract and hold love in your life.

How Environmental Conditions Affect Mental States

If you understand how the five elements (Water, Wood, Fire, Earth, Metal) act simultaneously in the inner (mental) and outer (environmental) dimensions, you will be able to see how, by adjusting the elements in your environment, you can bring about desired shifts in your experiences and fortunes in life. Putting this powerful method to practical use requires ascertaining two things: the elements of your personality and the elements in your environment. The elements of your personality are determined by Chinese astrology, and the elements in your environment are determined by compass directions.

It is obvious that we are all different. We all experience our environment in different ways. Because the elements of our personalities vary, you and I will have different experiences of the same space. Some of us have personalities with predominant Metal, some have predominant Water, some have Wood, some Fire, some Earth. Thus, there is no one way to do feng shui for everyone. People who claim to practice feng shui but do not apply Chinese astrological and compass methods are not practicing the authentic art. What you are receiving in this book is entirely authentic and powerful. If you give it your patient attention, you will have highly positive results.

Your Relationships

Just as your environment reflects your personal characteristics, your relationships mirror various aspects of your personality. A relationship is essentially a collective field. You and your partner spontaneously form a common psychic field when you become involved. In this field you naturally take sides, or assume polarized positions, in order to communicate and experience what you share in common. The richness and depth of this sharing determine the quality of your relationship.

In the largest sense, all sentient beings participate in a universal psychic field. This universal field, or world soul, is the background of our individual personalities. All ideas that we have, all that we believe about others, all that we see in others exists in our own minds as well as in the minds of everyone else. All is reflected in all. Not only is the world soul the origin of all soul mates but it enables us to learn from one another, understand one another, and attain universal knowledge by looking into our own hearts.

As each individual develops through life, certain characteristics become pronounced while others are forgotten. As we become individuals we go through a continual process in which we tell ourselves, "I am this; I am not that." Some of this process stems from our upbringing and social conditioning, and some is the result of our preconditioning. If we didn't have unique personalities, we all would be equally attracted to, and repelled by, everyone else at the same time. It is because of our unique personalities that our unique affinities and disaffinities exist.

We always find our complements. When life has brought you to the point that you are ready to be in an enduring love relationship, or marriage, it will happen. Notwithstanding, if you have unresolved inner conflicts, you will attract and be attracted to others who share your conflicts. It is only natural. Relationships in which you experience conflict can teach you much about yourself and help you evolve if you keep in mind that both sides of the conflict existing in the field of your relationship exist in your own mind as well. When you own both sides of the conflict and learn what it has to teach you, you will come to terms with and outgrow it. If you abandon a relationship in which you experience conflict without coming to terms with its origins in yourself, chances are that a variation of the same pattern will emerge in a future relationship.

The golden keys to having a relationship that works are self-knowledge and self-acceptance. Self-knowledge depends on self-reflection. In ancient China self-reflection was considered essential for harmonious relationships, extending from friendship, marriage, family, and community to the organization of the empire.

In the writings of the sages, the idea of self-reflection is characterized by the word *Te*. Ordinarily translated as "virtue," the Chinese character literally means action that results from looking directly into one's heart, or action that results from self-reflection, in other words, insightful action. Writing in the sixth century B.C.E. in *The Great Learning*, Confucius said,

> *Insightful action is the way of great learning. It depends on knowing where the point of stillness lies. When the point of stillness is found, the object of pursuit is determined, and calm fearlessness is gained. In that calmness is the repose and deliberation that leads to the attainment of the desired end.*
>
> *To know what is first and what is last will lead near to what is meant by the great learning. The ancients who wished to illustrate to the empire the nature of insightful action first set their own lands in order. Wishing to set their own lands in order, they first organized their families. Wishing to organize their families, they first cultivated themselves. Wishing to cultivate themselves, they first*

set right their hearts. Wishing to set right their hearts, they first sought to be sincere in their thoughts. Wishing to be sincere in their thoughts, they first sought to extend their knowledge to the utmost. Such extension of knowledge lies in the investigation of all things.

Things being investigated, their knowledge became complete. Their knowledge being complete, their thoughts became sincere. Their thoughts being sincere, their hearts were set right. Their hearts being set right, they were able to cultivate themselves. Being self-cultivated, their families became organized. Their families being organized, their lands were set in order. Their lands set in order, the entire empire was made peaceful and happy. From the head of state to the common people, all must consider self-cultivation as the root of everything. If the root is neglected, everything will become confused.

Considering how essential self-cultivation, or self-reflection, is to the development of a good relationship, it follows that choosing a place for this activity is the first practical step you should take in arranging the feng shui of your home. Relying on your intuitive sense, locate an area in your home where you will not be disturbed, a place where you can sit quietly, write in a journal, meditate, and dream. Let it be a place where you feel protected, comfortable, and happy. Clear it of all clutter. You may bring into it whatever personal objects, books, pictures, and articles of furniture you choose, or you can leave it empty. If you wish to, cut out Talisman 1 from the back of this book, mount and frame it, and place it in this special area as a reminder of your intention.

Exercises

- Make a list of your best points. You can start this in front of the mirror. Note your most attractive features and write them down. Next, note those things that might need a little work to improve the picture, but don't be too critical; a flaw often makes one all the more attractive. How would you describe your personality? How would you describe your occupation and aims in life? How would you describe your sense of humor? What makes you laugh? What kinds of music, art, or poetry do you enjoy? What kind of social life do you want to cultivate? What special interests do you have? How would you describe your sense of spirituality? There is no need to make your list terribly long. Give it some thought, however; it represents what you believe you have to offer of yourself in a relationship.

- Reflecting on your past love relationships, friendships, family relationships, and so forth, define the qualities you require in a partner. What do you need to feel safe and happy? Give some thought to this. From time to time you may want to revise your ideas.

- What are you willing to bring to a relationship? What are your ideas about commitment, integrity, responsibility, loyalty, personal freedom, intimacy, privacy, and so forth?

Your Yin or Yang Style of Relating

Before we begin discussing all the meanings of yin and yang, please fill out the following questionnaire. The results will reveal whether your style of relating, in a romantic sense, is yin or yang. For each question there are two possible responses. Mark the response that most applies to you.

The yin and yang attributes of your responses are listed after the questionnaire. Using that list, tally your responses. A majority of yin responses reveals that your romantic style of relating is yin; a majority of yang responses reveals that your romantic style of relating is yang. Be as spontaneous as possible in your responses. Your first thought is your best thought. If you are generally unsure, or if your tally reveals that you are equally yin and yang, wait until you have read Chapter 4 to decide which is your style of relating. Chapter 4 will reveal the yin-yang quality of the element of your day of birth.

Determining Your Yin-Yang Style of Relating

1. While engaging in a most interesting conversation with your best friend:

    a. you most naturally want to give all your observations and opinions.

    b. it is most natural for you to want to understand your friend's point of view.

2. Hoping to meet someone new, you have gone to a party with some friends. Someone attracts you from across the room. You want to meet him or her.
   a. You stare flirtatiously, hoping he or she will come over to you.
   b. You go over to him or her and say hello.

3. Your boyfriend or girlfriend, whom you really love, is showering you with gifts and cards as tokens of affection.
   a. You are beginning to feel smothered and annoyed by all this, and wish he or she would quit it and give you some breathing space.
   b. You are thrilled by all the attention; it reassures you of his or her love.

4. You are under a lot of pressure at work and are feeling stressed.
   a. You call up your girlfriend or boyfriend for moral support.
   b. You simply focus on solving the problems and forget about your feelings.

5. You have gone out shopping for clothes.
   a. You have decided what you need before going to the store, so you buy exactly what you want and then leave.
   b. You have a few ideas about things you might like to buy and go to the store to browse. When something appeals to you, you buy it.

6. You have been offered an exciting job opportunity in another city and want to take it. Much to your dismay, however, your girlfriend or boyfriend does not want to relocate because her or his friends and family are all here. After arguing for a long time about it:
   a. You decide to move by yourself, even if it means having to break off the relationship.
   b. You decide to give up the job opportunity for the sake of your relationship.

7. You have been in a committed relationship for months and agree to live together. You both have equally large and comfortable places. In light of this:
   a. You choose to move in with your lover.
   b. You want your lover to move in with you.

8. When planning a date with someone you have recently met:
   a. You offer suggestions of special places you think he or she might enjoy.
   b. You count on him or her to come up with suggestions so that you can choose a place you both agree upon.

9. You view a lifetime commitment more as:

   a. Taking a great responsibility upon yourself.

   b. Letting go of your independence.

10. You are having a wonderful conversation with someone you have just met. Hoping to see him or her again, you make a move to exchange telephone numbers by:

   a. Offering your number.

   b. Asking for his or her number.

11. You have been on a wonderful date with someone you recently met whom you find irresistible and who is obviously attracted to you too. Considering the circumstances:

   a. You think it is appropriate to go home to sleep together.

   b. You feel you would like to get to know him or her better before becoming intimate, because this could become an important relationship for you.

12. Your boyfriend or girlfriend is teaching you to drive.

   a. Even though you know he or she is helping you, you find yourself becoming irritated because you really don't like being told what to do.

   b. You follow his or her instructions easily because you respond positively to helpful guidance.

13. In the balance of your personality, which standpoint weighs more:

   a. You know what you want.

   b. You know what you don't want.

14. An ideal summer vacation for you would be:

   a. To go to a resort or arts festival in a beautiful natural setting with a large group of friends where you would enjoy many entertaining social and cultural events.

   b. To travel to foreign lands or wilderness in search of adventure.

15. Your lover wants you to go skydiving with her or him and some of her or his friends. The thought of skydiving makes you feel uneasy.

   a. You decline the invitation and suggest some things that both of you can enjoy together later on.

   b. You accept the invitation and make a show of courage because you know how good it feels to win your lover's admiration.

1. a. Yang	b. Yin	9. a. Yang	b. Yin
2. a. Yin	b. Yang	10. a. Yin	b. Yang
3. a. Yang	b. Yin	11. a. Yang	b. Yin
4. a. Yin	b. Yang	12. a. Yang	b. Yin
5. a. Yang	b. Yin	13. a. Yang	b. Yin
6. a. Yang	b. Yin	14. a. Yin	b. Yang
7. a. Yin	b. Yang	15. a. Yin	b. Yang
8. a. Yang	b. Yin		

In light of the popular misconception that men are yang and women are yin, it might have come as a surprise for you to discover that you are actually a yang woman or a yin man. Notwithstanding, if you think of yin and yang simply as qualities of energy, you will understand how it is that there can be both yin and yang men and women.

What Yin and Yang Are

Yin and yang are sometimes referred to as the two vital breaths of nature. Like the north and south poles of a magnet, they complement each other and are inseparable. In terms of the Tao, they are like two sides of a coin. Lao Tzu depicted them as a paradox when he wrote:

The Tao, when bright is dark;
When approaching, it retreats;
Its evenness seems to be uneven;
Its height is its depth;
Its greatest beauty is its ugliness;
Its wealth is its poverty;
Its strength is its weakness;
Its unchanging truth is change;

Its great squareness has no corners;
Its great potential takes forever to ripen;
Its great sound is its silence;
Its great form has no shape.

The Yin Energy Type

Yin energy is right-brained, imaginative, and feeling-centered. Yin energy type people prefer to follow. They love to communicate and share feelings. Because they are naturally interested in what has emotional appeal, things such as romantic stories, poetry, music, and art have special meaning for them. The yin type thrives when cherished and appreciated. If you are a yin type person, you are emotionally vulnerable. Your power lies in patient waiting, being self-protective, and knowing when to say no. Because you are inclined to know what you don't want more than what you do want, you tend to make important decisions by a process of elimination. It is characteristic of a yin type person to receive and to share.

The Yang Energy Type

Yang energy is left-brained, logical, concerned with facts, and attracted to power. Yang energy type people prefer to lead. They strive to gain control. They are naturally interested in objects, instruments, gadgets, statistics, the news, sports, making deals, and solving problems. A yang energy type hates to be given unsolicited advice or be told what to do. The yang type thrives when accepted and respected. If you are a yang type person, you are courageous. Your power lies in being able to initiate actions, to base your decisions on knowing what you want, to take responsibility, to protect those you love, and to be thoughtful and considerate of others. It is characteristic of a yang type person to give.

While reading these descriptions, you may have found that you identify with characteristics of both types. It also may be true that you can take the active, yang role in some areas of your life and the passive, yin role in others. This is perfectly natural. Considering that yin and yang are complementary expressions of the Tao, and that each and every one of us is a unique embodiment of the Tao, it is correct to observe that we all display both yin and yang characteristics. However, as our personalities unfold and we enter into relationships, we tend to polarize. Some of us naturally assume the yang role in personal relationships, and others of us naturally assume the yin role.

Yin and Yang in Relationship

Because yin and yang are mutually complementary and attracted to each other, it is essential to know where you stand if you want to have a relationship that works. If your style of relating is yin, you will get along most successfully with a yang partner. By contrast, if your style of relating is yang, you will get along most successfully with someone who is yin.

In a romantic relationship where both partners are either yin or yang, serious problems develop. If both partners are yin, both will want to follow. Because each will need the other to take the lead, their relationship will become confused, lose all sense of direction, and fizzle out. If both partners are yang, both will want to take the lead. Because neither will agree to follow the other, they will compete with each other, interrupt each other in conversations, quarrel, and break up.

Not only should you know where you stand but you need to maintain your yin or yang style consistently, especially through the first few months of your relationship. Shifting polarities, or roles, without mutual agreement can sabotage a relationship. If you are uncertain of yourself, if you habitually vacillate between yin and yang roles, or if you try to play both at once, you will make it extremely difficult, if not impossible, to have a relationship that works. Remember, a relationship is a field whose contents two people share by taking complementary sides. One has to assume the north, or yin, pole, and the other has to assume the south, or yang, pole for the current to flow freely between them.

In the long run, in a healthy and enduring relationship, the yin and yang balance between partners tends to become highly sophisticated, especially when the strengths of one compensate for the weaknesses of the other. As your relationship evolves you may find yourself taking the yin role in one area and the yang role in another. The yin and yang forces, both in your individual personality and in your relationship, will always seek to balance and complement each other. This is a natural principle.

Balancing the Yin and Yang Aspects of Your Home

An environment whose yin and yang functions are harmoniously related promotes feelings of well-being. The yin and yang aspects of your home include things such as its common and private areas, open and enclosed areas, larger and smaller rooms, light and shade, warm and cool colors, and so forth. In summary, we have the following:

Yin	Yang
Private areas	Common areas
Back rooms	Front rooms
Smaller rooms	Larger rooms
Enclosed areas	Open areas
Shade	Light
Cool colors	Warm colors
Subdued colors	Vivid colors
Carpeted floors	Bare floors
Informal arrangements	Formal arrangements

Although we will discuss ways of working with the yin and yang aspects of your home in detail in Part Two, begin to become aware of them now. Note the balance of colors and light in your home. Imagine how you might arrange your home to balance its more common areas with its private areas using furniture arrangements and colors. Consider the different levels, and interplay, of your home's light and shade, and how you might use lighting to create focal points, like pools, and imaginary pathways, like streams.

While people are attracted to light, diffused lighting will drive people apart.

You can balance light and shade to make intimate sitting areas more inviting. If your home is too brightly lit, it will not draw people together.

There is a beautiful Chinese verse alluding to marriage that describes the interaction of yin and yang. It says, "The interactions of the natural forces produce the harmony of the universe." You will find this verse in Talisman 2 in the back of this book. In Part Two, I will show you where to place this talisman, which is a good-luck charm.

Exercise

In your Personal Data list, write down your yin or yang style of relating. If you are unsure of it, wait until you have read Chapter 4. The astrological information there will decide the matter for you.

Water, Wood, Fire, Earth, or Metal

Let's begin our exploration of the five elements with another questionnaire. This way you will be able to determine empirically which of the elements is most pronounced in your life at present without any preconceptions about what the elements mean.

The questionnaire actually consists of forty-five statements. In the blank to the left of each statement, indicate the degree to which you identify with it by rating it as follows:

0 = Never true
1 = Seldom true
2 = Occasionally true
3 = Often true
4 = Always true

Fill out the questionnaire completely, and with as little deliberation as possible. Remember, your first thought is your best thought.

Determining Your Most Favored Element

____ 1. Because I am flexible, it is easy for me to adapt to most circumstances.

____ 2. I tend to be impulsive and impatient with other people's misgivings.

____ 3. The way I and other people look is very important to me.

____ 4. I tend to be critical and obsessive over details.

____ 5. When I set standards for myself, I expect others to measure up to them as well.

____ 6. I tend to be fascinated by people, things, and places that are mysterious.

____ 7. My favorite color is green, bright blue, or turquoise.

____ 8. I have expensive tastes and love to spend freely on things such as fine furniture, clothes, jewelry, and art objects.

____ 9. I tend to be very cautious in my financial and business dealings.

____ 10. In social relations, I value tact and decorum most highly.

____ 11. Even though I might appear to be calm and easygoing, I tend to fret and experience dark moods.

____ 12. I love challenges and adventures.

____ 13. I am very vulnerable to cold weather.

____ 14. I am very concerned about the needs and feelings of my loved ones.

____ 15. Because I aim to be the best, I work hard and relentlessly at everything I do.

____ 16. Because I have strong powers of concentration, I am an excellent detective.

____ 17. Because I pursue my desires passionately, I become angry when I feel thwarted.

____ 18. My favorite color is red, purple, rose, or pink.

____ 19. Because I need to belong and be helpful to others, I tend to be a conformist.

____ 20. I suffer from skin problems, dry skin and hair, respiratory problems, or sinus problems.

____ 21. It is easy for me to conceal my intentions while appearing to be open and outgoing.

23

___ 22. Although I am a romantic and fall in love easily, love often spells trouble for me.

___ 23. While I love to be in the limelight, I do not let others invade my privacy.

___ 24. My favorite color is yellow, gold, orange, brown, tan, or beige.

___ 25. I have a highly refined sense of aesthetics and hate disorder.

___ 26. My favorite color is black or dark blue.

___ 27. I have excellent coordination, am very agile, and love speed.

___ 28. I love to be entertained and laugh a lot.

___ 29. My tendency to worry gives me a nervous stomach.

___ 30. My favorite color is white, gray, or silver.

___ 31. I am a pack rat; I hate to throw anything out.

___ 32. I work hard at defining goals and far-reaching plans for my future.

___ 33. Because I experience extremes of joy and anguish in love, I tend to be possessive and react angrily when I feel rejected.

___ 34. Because it takes me a long time to make up my mind, I get involved slowly.

___ 35. I suffer from grief.

___ 36. While I have intense sexual desires and passions, I fear losing myself in others.

___ 37. I suffer from migratory pains, hypertension, or tendonitis or have brittle fingernails.

___ 38. I tend to have a hectic lifestyle.

___ 39. Because I do not want to offend anyone, I am gentle and discreet with others.

___ 40. I am willing to take great risks for high stakes.

___ 41. I have trouble sleeping.

___ 42. I am high-spirited, optimistic, and aspiring.

___ 43. I am spontaneous and volatile, and have brilliant flashes of insight.

___ 44. I experience torpor, lethargy, and indifference.

___ 45. I use my subtle abilities to sense other people's feelings to influence them.

How to Tally Your Answers

The numbered blanks following each element correspond to the questions you have just answered. Transfer your questionnaire answers to their corresponding blanks. For example, if your answer to question 4 was 0, write a 0 in the blank next to 4, the first blank under Earth. When you have filled in all of your answers, add up the numbers under each element. The element with the highest number is your favored element.

Water	Wood	Fire	Earth	Metal
__ 1.	__ 2.	__ 3.	__ 4.	__ 5.
__ 6.	__ 7.	__ 8.	__ 9.	__ 10.
__ 11.	__ 12.	__ 13.	__ 14.	__ 15.
__ 16.	__ 17.	__ 18.	__ 19.	__ 20.
__ 21.	__ 22.	__ 23.	__ 24.	__ 25.
__ 26.	__ 27.	__ 28.	__ 29.	__ 30.
__ 31.	__ 32.	__ 33.	__ 34.	__ 35.
__ 36.	__ 37.	__ 38.	__ 39.	__ 40.
__ 41.	__ 42.	__ 43.	__ 44.	__ 45.
__ TOTAL	__ TOTAL	__ TOTAL	__ TOTAL	__ TOTAL

Your favored element is like a window that reveals an important aspect of your personality at this time of your life. If your tally reveals that you have two equally favored elements, read the descriptions of both.

When reading the following descriptions, please bear in mind that they do not represent the full picture of your personality. The full picture will be revealed over this and the next few chapters.

The Characteristics of Water

Water as your favored element indicates that your thoughts, emotions, and physical energy fluctuate like the moon and the tides of the sea. You may experience periods of buoyant moods followed by periods of cold and somber moods. Your inner and outer bearing are often diametrically opposed. While you feel inwardly restless, you can appear perfectly calm and composed. Conversely, you can be perfectly serene in the midst of hectic activity. You can also be outgoing and ebullient while keeping your true thoughts to yourself. This dual proclivity of yours, coupled with your love for the mysterious, makes you quite a private eye and natural psychic. Deep thought and reflection are your strong points. Therefore, in arranging the feng shui of your home, provide yourself with a place for privacy and calm reflection.

The Characteristics of Wood

If Wood is your favored element, you aspire in thought, emotions, and physical energy like the trees that reach up to the sun. Because it is essential for you to grow and develop, you are naturally drawn to new ideas, opportunities, and horizons. It is your interest in what is new that keeps you forever youthful. You are naturally kindhearted and gentle, and are full of surprises. You are inventive and have talents for designing and planning. Your creativity and romantic intelligence are your strong points. Therefore, in arranging the feng shui of your home, provide yourself with a space, like a study, for your books, music, and works of art where you can concentrate and pursue your creative aims.

The Characteristics of Fire

If Fire is your favored element, your thoughts, emotions, and physical energy are expansive and warm, like the sun that shines upon the whole world. You love to be entertained and are fun-loving and friendly to many people. Yet few ever get close enough to really know you. You are something of a paradox. You can be warm and sensual on the one hand, proud and distant on the other. You love all that is gorgeous and grand, and will go to great lengths to live in opulent surroundings. You have expensive tastes and are tempted to live beyond your means. Your artistic and intuitive abilities, as well as your capacity for joy, are your strong points. Therefore, in arranging the feng shui of your home, make it a gorgeous place. It should be filled with beautiful furniture, carpets, and works of art. Your home should be a place you love to be in, whether you are alone, with your sweetheart, or throwing a party for all your friends.

The Characteristics of Earth

If Earth is your favored element, your thoughts, emotions, and physical energy are slow to change and well-grounded, like the earth upon which we live. Because security is so important to you, you are generally careful and considerate, and are happy when others depend on you for help. You tend to be devoted to those you love. You are reliable, detail-oriented, firm, and enduring. Your concerns and interests include down-to-earth matters such as money, food, health, home, and family matters. Your kindness, tolerance, and ability to nurture others are your strong points. Therefore, in arranging the feng shui of your home, make it a warm and comfortable place. Ideally, it should have a big, comfortable kitchen.

The Characteristics of Metal

Metal, as your favored element, shows that your thoughts, emotions, and physical energy are keen and tempered like fine steel. You are highly idealistic and dignified, and have excellent abilities to communicate your ideas and inspire others. You are keenly perceptive, capable of subtlety, decisive in action, and graceful in spirit; you calculate your moves. You have acute senses and fine tastes, and are attracted to all that is elegant and aristocratic. Your intellectual and creative abilities and your sense of order are your strong points. Therefore, in arranging the feng shui of your home, make it elegant and orderly. Provide yourself with a fine library or study—a place where you can think undisturbed.

Exercise

In your Personal Data list, enter your favored element or elements, and what it or they mean in terms of arranging the feng shui of your home.

chapter 4

Your Basic Personality Type, Relationship Element, and Element of Mutual Harmony

In the system of astrology used in this book, the five elements are divided into yin and yang forms to produce ten basic personality types. These ten types are called yin Water, yang Water, yin Wood, yang Wood, yin Fire, yang Fire, yin Earth, yang Earth, yin Metal, and yang Metal. The meaning of these types is different from what you read in Chapter 3. As you will recall, your favored element reveals an important aspect of your personality at this time of your life. Your personality type, however, is something you were born with. It is basic to your nature and, as you grow older, exerts a more and more constant influence in your life. In order to determine your all-important personality type, read the following instructions carefully. Make sure you understand them.

How to Determine Your Personality Type

You will find a table and a wheel on the following pages. The table, Yin-Yang Qualities and Elements, contains the yin-yang quality and element for the first of January of each year from 1929 through 2019. Beside each leap year you will see an asterisk (*). The Wheel of Yin-Yang Qualities and Elements contains the ten personality types, arranged clockwise.

1. In the table find the yin-yang quality and element for the first of January of the year in which you were born and mark its corresponding yin-yang quality and element position on the wheel.

2. Count the number of days from and including January 1st up to and including the day of your birth. Here are the number of days for each month:

January = 31	July = 31
February = 28 (29 in leap year)	August = 31
March = 31	September = 30
April = 30	October = 31
May = 31	November = 30
June = 30	December = 31

3. Divide the number you obtained in step 2 by 10.

4. Discard the quotient and keep the remainder. (For example, 93 divided by 10 = 9 with 3 left over. Therefore, the 9 is the quotient, the 3 is the remainder, so you will discard the 9 and keep the 3.) Please note, the remainder can be any number from 0 to 9. (For example, 10 divided by 10 = 1 with 0 left over.)

5. Take your remainder to the wheel and, beginning at your marked position, count clockwise as many positions as your remainder indicates. Your marked position on the wheel always counts as position 1.

   If your remainder is 1, your personality type is indicated by your marked position on the wheel. If your remainder is 0, however, count counterclockwise one step from your marked position to determine your personality type.

Yin-Yang Qualities and Elements

January Ist	Yin-Yang Quality	Element
1929	Yang	Fire
1930	Yin	Metal
1931	Yang	Fire
1932*	Yin	Metal
1933	Yin	Fire
1934	Yang	Water
1935	Yin	Fire
1936*	Yang	Water

January 1st	Yin-Yang Quality	Element
1937	Yang	Earth
1938	Yin	Water
1939	Yang	Earth
1940*	Yin	Water
1941	Yin	Earth
1942	Yang	Wood
1943	Yin	Earth
1944*	Yang	Wood
1945	Yang	Metal
1946	Yin	Wood
1947	Yang	Metal
1948*	Yin	Wood
1949	Yin	Metal
1950	Yang	Fire
1951	Yin	Metal
1952*	Yang	Fire
1953	Yang	Water
1954	Yin	Fire
1955	Yang	Water
1956*	Yin	Fire
1957	Yin	Water
1958	Yang	Earth
1959	Yin	Water
1960*	Yang	Earth
1961	Yang	Wood
1962	Yin	Earth
1963	Yang	Wood
1964*	Yin	Earth
1965	Yin	Wood
1966	Yang	Metal
1967	Yin	Wood
1968*	Yang	Metal
1969	Yang	Fire
1970	Yin	Metal
1971	Yang	Fire

January 1st	Yin-Yang Quality	Element
1972*	Yin	Metal
1973	Yin	Fire
1974	Yang	Water
1975	Yin	Fire
1976*	Yang	Water
1977	Yang	Earth
1978	Yin	Water
1979	Yang	Earth
1980*	Yin	Water
1981	Yin	Earth
1982	Yang	Wood
1983	Yin	Earth
1984*	Yang	Wood
1985	Yang	Metal
1986	Yin	Wood
1987	Yang	Metal
1988*	Yin	Wood
1989	Yin	Metal
1990	Yang	Fire
1991	Yin	Metal
1992*	Yang	Fire
1993	Yang	Water
1994	Yin	Fire
1995	Yang	Water
1996*	Yin	Fire
1997	Yin	Water
1998	Yang	Earth
1999	Yin	Water
2000*	Yang	Earth
2001	Yang	Wood
2002	Yin	Earth
2003	Yang	Wood
2004*	Yin	Earth
2005	Yin	Wood
2006	Yang	Metal

January 1st	Yin-Yang Quality	Element
2007	Yin	Wood
2008*	Yang	Metal
2009	Yang	Fire
2010	Yin	Metal
2011	Yang	Fire
2012*	Yin	Metal
2013	Yin	Fire
2014	Yang	Water
2015	Yin	Fire
2016*	Yang	Water
2017	Yang	Earth
2018	Yin	Water
2019	Yang	Earth

The Wheel of Yin-Yang Qualities and Elements

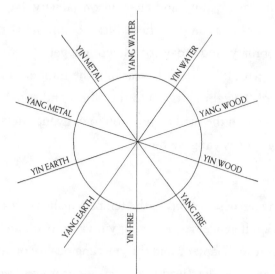

Here are three examples to demonstrate the method.

▪ Let's say that you were born on April 18th, 1965. We first note that the yin-yang quality and element for January 1st, 1965, is yin Wood, then mark yin

Wood on the wheel. Next, since there are 31 days in January, 28 days in February, 31 days in March, and 18 days up to and including April 18th, we add these and get 108. Next, we divide 108 by 10 and get 10 with 8 left over. Discarding the quotient of 10, and keeping the remainder of 8, we bring the 8 to the wheel and, starting at the marked position, count 8 steps clockwise, which brings us to yang Water. Thus, your personality type is yang Water.

- To find the personality type for John, born on July 19th, 1972, we first note that the yin-yang quality and element on January 1st, 1972, is yin Metal then mark yin Metal on the wheel. Next, since there are 31 days in January, 29 days in February (1972 being a leap year), 31 days in March, 30 days in April, 31 days in May, 30 days in June, and 19 days in July up to and including the 19th, we add these up and get 201. Next, we divide 201 by 10 and get 20 with 1 left over. Discarding the quotient of 20 and keeping the remainder of 1, we bring the 1 to the wheel. Then, counting the marked position as 1, we learn that John's personality type is yin Metal.

- To find the personality type for Sarah, born March 1st, 1970, we first note that the yin-yang quality and element on January 1st, 1970, is yin Metal, then mark yin Metal on the wheel. Next, counting 31 days for January, 28 days for February, and 1 day for March, we get 60. Next, we divide 60 by 10 to get 6 with 0 left over. Discarding the quotient of 6 and keeping the remainder of 0, we bring the 0 to the wheel and count one position counterclockwise from the marked position to get yang Metal. Therefore Sarah's personality type is yang Metal.

The following are descriptions of the ten personality types. If you have discovered that there is a difference between your yin-yang style of relating as determined by the questionnaire in Chapter 2 and the yin-yang quality of your personality type, don't let this confuse you. Just read the description of your personality type here. Later in this chapter I will show you how your yin-yang style of relating comes into play in determining your relationship element.

The Romantic Characteristics
of the Ten Personality Types

- If you were born on a day of yin Water, there is something calm and mysterious about you. You might even appear to be cool and indifferent. Nonetheless, the force of your sexual desire and magnetism tend to draw you inevitably into passions that are nearly impossible for you to undo. In the earlier stages of dating it is natural for you to play hard to get and to carry on secret flirtations with several people at the same time. But when you become emotionally and sexually involved, you change completely; you become deeply attached and won't let go. The colors that correspond to your personal element are black and deep blues.

- If you were born on a day of yang Water, you have the ability to turn the desires and passions of others to your advantage. Because you are secretive, willful, seductive, and attracted to power, you fascinate others. You respond readily to flirtation and make an enthusiastic lover. Monogamy, however, is not natural to you. You will not feel comfortable in a monogamous relationship unless your partner adapts to your way and is sexually highly compatible with you. The colors that correspond to your personal element are black and deep blues.

- If you were born on a day of yin Wood, your nature is variable like the wind. You are inclined to change your mind again and again, because you tend to be indecisive, anxious about the future, and extremely sensitive to the things people say to you. You can also be quite whimsical and adventurous. Because you are usually open-minded and communicative, you are at your best in a relationship with someone who is an engaging and resourceful conversationalist. You are inclined to believe that others are as kindhearted as you. This belief can cause you a lot of trouble, not only because it puts you at a disadvantage but because it hinders you from understanding those you love so tenderly. The colors that correspond to your personal element are greens and the lighter shades of blue.

- If you were born on a day of yang Wood, you are naturally independent and upbeat. Your optimistic and high-spirited ways make you lovable and fun to be with. You can be most talkative and engaging, and get yourself into plenty of trouble by saying things you shouldn't; it's hard for you to keep secrets. Because you are so impulsive, you tend to fall in love easily, even suddenly, and can become quite blinded by it. You are surely one of the favorites of Cupid! Unfortunately, when things don't work out the way you want, you have the greatest difficulty realizing the truth, let alone listening to advice. Because you hate to take no for an answer, you can be deeply wounded by rejections. But if you are cut down, you spring back to life. Because you are a true romantic, hope springs eternal for you. The colors that correspond to your personal element are greens and the lighter shades of blue.

- If you were born on a day of yin Fire, you are warmhearted, sensuous, and playful. You are also artistically inclined and attracted to all that is beautiful and luxurious. You love to entertain and can easily attract a large circle of friends and admirers. Few people, however, will ever become intimate with you. You are something of an actor who has a very private life. While you can be seductive with gestures and words, you tend to have high expectations of those you attract. If you are disappointed by them, you lose interest and move on quickly. While this sort of behavior can win you the reputation of being fickle, you're not. Once you fall in love you become intensely devoted, even jealous. Those who are close to you know you have a heart filled with love. The colors that correspond to your personal element are reds, purples, roses, and pinks.

- If you were born on a day of yang Fire, you want to be the best, to play the leading role, and to be the center of attention. You are a gifted speaker who, with your sexy voice and choice words, can melt anyone's heart. You have keen perceptions and feelings, and are very playful. Notwithstanding, you are proud and impulsive, and can humiliate those you poke fun at; you have a sharp tongue. You can also appear to be cold and distant, holding all you disdain at arm's length. Nevertheless, because you are sensuous and passionate, you thrive on love and are happiest when you have someone in your life who absolutely adores you. You may go through a period in life when you reject one lover after another. But when the right one shows up you become very loyal, if not possessive. The colors that correspond to your personal element are reds, purples, roses, and pinks.

- If you were born on a day of yin Earth, you are gentle and caring, nurturing and supportive, and are attracted to old-fashioned values that make for a secure, comfortable, and productive way in life. You are family-oriented and take pride in being true to your word and faithful in your commitments. You are generally shy and reserved, and attracted to strong, assertive types. It is natural for you to choose your partner by how you feel rather than what you think about him or her. You have definite likes and dislikes, and little, if any, trouble showing your preferences. In love you are devoted. You are very sensitive and aware of subtle nuances of feeling. Be careful not to let your sensitivity give way to fussing over details, however. Worrying will not make you happy. The colors that correspond to your personal element are yellows, golds, oranges, browns, tans, and beiges.

- If you were born on a day of yang Earth, you are the strong, silent type. While you normally appear gentle and peaceful, you are strong-willed and independent, and, because you are intent upon having your way, can become reactive and argumentative even to the point of alienating your friends. You could be called the rugged individualist. You have strong desires that you don't like to show, not that you are secretive; you are actually very honest when push comes to shove. While you are loyal in love, it takes time for you to choose your mate. You could go through a few affairs before you decide. Once you make up your mind, however, you will let nothing get in the way of making good your intentions. Because you are attracted to marriage, you have no trouble making and keeping commitments. When settled in marriage you become tolerant, protective, and respectful of your mate. You value honesty and loyalty most highly in love. The colors that correspond to your personal element are yellows, golds, oranges, browns, tans, and beiges.

- If you were born on a day of yin Metal, you are freedom-loving, sociable, pleasure-seeking, and artistic. You are gifted with an intuitive awareness of other people's moods and the ability to sway them with your words and subtle gestures. Because you know how to please others, and somehow manage always to look good, others are drawn to you. You can easily attract a large and interesting circle of friends, who share your tastes and show you the kind of attention you love to receive. The worst thing in the world for you is to be ignored. You cannot bear to be alone and instinctively look for companionship. Indeed, much of your success in life depends on whether you have someone to love you and give you emotional support. You are far less motivated when alone than in a relationship. Notwithstanding, your love of freedom lets you easily get out of what you get into, so you can have a number of significant relationships rather than marrying. The right choice, however, when made intelligently, will bring you great happiness and contentment. The colors that correspond to your personal element are whites, grays, and silver.

- If you were born on a day of yang Metal, you put yourself wholeheartedly into whatever you do, and, while you like to appear independent and self-contained, you have a profound need for true love. In courtship you characteristically take the lead and pursue your ideal of love without reserve. If it turns out that the object of your affection is not capable of the devotion and commitment you require, you can easily change your focus and either entertain superficial involvements with several people at once or direct your attentions to other matters and remain completely alone for as long as you wish. You need to be careful not to let your would-be sweethearts take unfair advantage of your penchant for being helpful and generous. For you to be happy in a relationship, you must strike a perfect balance between independence and loyalty. Trust and complete acceptance are essential for your love to flourish. The colors that correspond to your personal element are whites, grays, and silver.

Your Relationship Element

Your relationship element is your most important key to your personal colors and compass directions, especially for aligning your bed. In order to determine your relationship element, you will need to take into account your yin-yang style of relating, as determined in Chapter 2, plus your personal element, as just determined. Please note the following:

- If your yin-yang style of relating differs from the yin-yang quality of your personal element, use the style of relating rather than the quality of your personal element and read the appropriate descriptive paragraph. For example, if your style of relating is yang but you were born on the day of yin Wood, read the paragraph that begins, "If you are yang and Wood."
- If you were undecided about your yin-yang style of relating, or found that your score on the questionnaire in Chapter 2 was inconclusive, simply read the paragraph that corresponds to your personal element. For example, if you were born on the day of yin Wood, read the paragraph that begins, "If you are yin and Wood."

If you are yin and Water, your relationship element is Earth. The corresponding directions in space for Earth are southwest and northeast. The colors for Earth are the yellows, golds, oranges, browns, tans, and beiges.

If you are yang and Water, your relationship element is Fire. The corresponding direction in space for Fire is south. The colors for Fire are the reds, purples, roses, and pinks.

If you are yin and Wood, your relationship element is Metal. The corresponding directions in space for Metal are west and northwest. The colors for Metal are the whites, grays, and silver.

If you are yang and Wood, your relationship element is Earth. The corresponding directions in space for Earth are southwest and northeast. The colors for Earth are the yellows, golds, oranges, browns, tans, and beiges.

If you are yin and Fire, your relationship element is Water. The corresponding direction in space for Water is north. The colors for Water are black and the deeper shades of blue.

If you are yang and Fire, your relationship element is Metal. The corresponding directions in space for Metal are west and northwest. The colors for Metal are the whites, grays, and silver.

If you are yin and Earth, your relationship element is Wood. The corresponding directions in space for Wood are east and southeast. The colors for Wood are the greens and the lighter shades of blue.

If you are yang and Earth, your relationship element is Water. The corresponding direction in space for Water is north. The colors for Water are black and the darker shades of blue.

If you are yin and Metal, your relationship element is Fire. The corresponding direction in space for Fire is south. The colors for Fire are the reds, purples, roses, and pinks.

If you are yang and Metal, your relationship element is Wood. The corresponding directions in space for Wood are east and southeast. The colors for Wood are the greens and the lighter shades of blue.

Your Element of Mutual Harmony

If you live together as a couple, you probably don't have an identical relationship element. If your two relationship elements are not the same, you still can use them for various details in arranging the feng shui of your home. However, they will not work for the compass alignment of your bed. For this reason you need to combine your personal element with your partner's to find your element or elements of mutual harmony. After using the table of the elements of mutual harmony, refer to the table of compass and color correspondences to find the directions in space and color choices for your element or elements of mutual harmony. Finally, enter this information in your Personal Data list.

You will notice that some combinations yield two or even three elements of mutual harmony. This will give you a greater range of alignment and color possibilities. For example, if your personal element is Wood and your partner's personal element is Fire, your elements of mutual harmony are Wood and Fire.

If you and your partner have the same relationship element, you can use either it or your element or elements of mutual harmony to align your bed.

Elements of Mutual Harmony

Combination	Elements of Mutual Harmony
Water and Water	Water, Metal, and Wood
Water and Wood	Water and Wood
Water and Fire	Wood
Water and Earth	Metal
Water and Metal	Water and Metal
Wood and Wood	Wood, Water, and Fire
Wood and Fire	Wood and Fire
Wood and Earth	Fire
Wood and Metal	Water
Fire and Fire	Fire, Wood, and Earth
Fire and Earth	Fire and Earth
Fire and Metal	Earth
Earth and Earth	Earth, Fire, and Metal
Earth and Metal	Earth and Metal
Metal and Metal	Metal, Earth, and Water

Compass and Color Correspondences

Element	Directions in Space	Colors
Water	North	Black and deep blues
Wood	East and southeast	Greens and light blues
Fire	South	Reds, purples, roses, pinks
Earth	Southwest and northeast	Yellows, golds, oranges, browns, tans, beiges
Metal	West and northwest	Whites, grays, silver

The following vignette illustrates how to use this method.

Fran and Larry

Fran and Larry live together. Fran's personal element is Fire, and Larry's is Water. Looking at the table of the elements of mutual harmony, they find that their element of mutual harmony is Wood. Looking then at the table of compass and color correspondences, they find that the best directions in which to align their bed are east and southeast, and that they can use greens and the lighter shades of blue to support the harmony of their relationship.

I will show you the complete method for using this information in Part Two. In the meantime you can wear a ring or other piece of jewelry with a stone whose color is that of your relationship element as a personal love charm. For example, if Fire is your relationship element, you could wear a ruby, garnet, or amethyst ring to attract love.

Exercise

If you have not done so yet, enter the following in your Personal Data list:

- Your personal element (personality type) and its corresponding colors.
- Your partner's personal element and its corresponding colors, if you are living together.
- Your relationship element with its corresponding direction or directions in space and colors.
- Your partner's relationship element with its corresponding direction or directions in space and colors.
- Your element or elements of mutual harmony with their corresponding direction or directions in space and colors.

Your Area of Special Interest

In Chapter 3 you read some of the characteristics of your favored element. In this chapter we will discuss how your favored element relates to your personal element as determined in Chapter 4.

If you view your favored element from the standpoint of your personal element, it reveals your area of special interest. Whether it signifies friendships, professional and financial interests, matters of social status, education, and so forth, your area of special interest is something that you cannot afford to neglect if you want to be at peace with yourself and your relationship. Because this element is important to your integrity and happiness, it represents something you might wish to give space in your home.

To access your area of special interest, first locate the heading in this section that corresponds to your personal element. Then find the item under that heading that corresponds to your favored element. For example, if your personal element is Wood and your favored element is Earth, you first would look to the heading "If Your Personal Element Is Wood," then go to the item under that heading that begins, "Earth as your favored element."

If Your Personal Element Is Water

- Water as your favored element indicates that your area of special interest involves self-knowledge, friendships, and relationships with brothers and sisters.
- Wood as your favored element indicates that your area of special interest involves your career, work, and creative projects.
- Fire as your favored element indicates that your area of special interest involves financial matters and acquisition of property.
- Earth as your favored element indicates that your area of special interest involves your social status and fame or reputation.
- Metal as your favored element indicates that your area of special interest involves education and research, as well as relationships with teachers, mentors, and guides.

If Your Personal Element Is Wood

- Wood as your favored element indicates that your area of special interest involves self-knowledge, friendships, and relationships with brothers and sisters.
- Fire as your favored element indicates that your area of special interest involves your career, work, and creative projects.
- Earth as your favored element indicates that your area of special interest involves financial matters and acquisition of property.
- Metal as your favored element indicates that your area of special interest involves your social status and fame or reputation.
- Water as your favored element indicates that your area of special interest involves education and research, as well as relationships with teachers, mentors, and guides.

If Your Personal Element Is Fire

- Fire as your favored element indicates that your area of special interest involves self-knowledge, friendships, and relationships with brothers and sisters.
- Earth as your favored element indicates that your area of special interest involves your career, work, and creative projects.
- Metal as your favored element indicates that your area of special interest involves financial matters and acquisition of property.
- Water as your favored element indicates that your area of special interest involves your social status and fame or reputation.
- Wood as your favored element indicates that your area of special interest involves education and research, as well as relationships with teachers, mentors, and guides.

If Your Personal Element Is Earth

- Earth as your favored element indicates that your area of special interest involves self-knowledge, friendships, and relationships with brothers and sisters.
- Metal as your favored element indicates that your area of special interest involves your career, work, and creative projects.
- Water as your favored element indicates that your area of special interest involves financial matters and acquisition of property.
- Wood as your favored element indicates that your area of special interest involves your social standing and fame or reputation.
- Fire as your favored element indicates that your area of special interest involves education and research, as well as relationships with teachers, mentors, and guides.

If Your Personal Element Is Metal

- Metal as your favored element indicates that your area of special interest involves self-knowledge, friendships, and relationships with brothers and sisters.

- Water as your favored element indicates that your area of special interest involves your career, work, and creative projects.

- Wood as your favored element indicates that your area of special interest involves financial matters and acquisition of property.

- Fire as your favored element indicates that your area of special interest involves your social standing and fame or reputation.

- Earth as your favored element indicates that your area of special interest involves education and research, as well as relationships with teachers, mentors, and guides.

Concerning your area of special interest for arranging your home, there are two things to consider. The first is translating your area of special interest into an actual space. The second is ascertaining the colors and compass directions that correspond to your area of special interest. Let's look at each.

Providing Space for Your Area of Special Interest

- If your area of special interest includes self-knowledge, friendships, and relationships with brothers and sisters, provide yourself with a private area for self-reflection and journaling. Also arrange a comfortable area in your home where your friends, brothers, and sisters can enjoy visiting you. This area could be your living room, or your kitchen if it is sufficiently comfortable and roomy.

- If your area of special interest involves your career, work, and creative projects, provide yourself with a private area, like a home office or studio, for your career planning and creative activities.

- If your area of special interest involves financial matters and acquisition of property, provide yourself with a private area or home office for your financial planning and storage of private files.
- If your area of special interest involves your social status and fame or reputation, provide yourself with a private area or home office devoted to your professional affairs and arrange your dining area and living room so that you can entertain in style.
- If your area of special interest involves education and research, as well as relationships with teachers, mentors, and guides, provide yourself with an area or room for a library and private study.

Corresponding Colors and Directions

- If your area of special interest is indicated by Water, its corresponding colors are black and the deeper shades of blue. Its corresponding direction in space is north.
- If your area of special interest is indicated by Wood, its corresponding colors are all shades of green and the lighter shades of blue. Its corresponding directions in space are east and southeast.
- If your area of special interest is indicated by Fire, its corresponding colors are all shades of red, purple, rose, and pink. Its corresponding direction in space is south.
- If your area of special interest is indicated by Earth, its corresponding colors are all shades of yellow, gold, orange, brown, tan, and beige. Its corresponding directions in space are southwest and northeast.
- If your area of special interest is indicated by Metal, its corresponding colors are all shades of white, gray, and silver. Its corresponding directions in space are west and northwest.

In Part Two, when we discuss the actual arrangement of your home, I will show you how to incorporate this information. At this stage it is only necessary for you to gather it.

Exercise

- According to the relation between your personal element and favored element, what is your area of special interest? Enter it in your Personal Data list.
- How can you provide for your area of special interest in arranging your home? Enter this information in your Personal Data list.
- Enter the corresponding colors and directions in space for your area of special interest in your Personal Data list.
- If you live together, can you find out your partner's area of special interest? If so, enter it in your Personal Data list.
- How can you provide for your partner's area of special interest in arranging your home? Enter this information in your Personal Data list.
- Enter the corresponding colors and directions in space for your partner's area of special interest in your Personal Data list.

Your Full Portrait in Chinese Astrology

We are ready now to fill out the details of your personal portrait by taking up the element and animal signs of your year and day of birth. When you combine these with what you have gathered in the preceding chapters, a clear astrological picture of your personality, relationships, and personal feng shui requirements will emerge.

There are twelve animal signs: Rat, Ox, Tiger, Rabbit, Dragon, Snake, Horse, Sheep, Monkey, Rooster, Dog, and Pig. These signs are combined with the five elements to produce sixty types. The sixty types are characterized by names such as Wood Rat, Fire Tiger, Earth Dragon, Metal Horse, and Water Monkey.

No doubt you have heard people say, "Oh, I'm a Dragon," "I'm a Metal Pig," or some such thing. What they are really saying is that they were born in the year of the Dragon or Metal Pig, and that these signs reveal something about their personalities. While this certainly is true, we mustn't ignore the assertion of Chinese astrologers that to obtain an accurate reading of your personality, especially with regard to your love life, you have to look at the combination of the element and animal signs of your year and day of birth, giving greater emphasis to the element and animal sign of your day of birth.

The element and animal sign of your year of birth reveals the basic substance, or background, of your personality. The element and animal sign of your day of birth reveals that into which your personality develops through your life. If we describe this relation using the metaphor of a gold statue of a lion, the element and animal sign of your year of birth is like the gold, while the element and animal sign of your day of birth is like the figure of the lion into which the gold has been shaped. The first is the material; the second is the form it takes.

Determining the Element and Animal Sign of Your Year of Birth

Use the following table of yearly elements and animal signs to find the element and animal sign of your birth year. The year dates in this table follow the Chinese lunar calendar. You will notice that the Chinese new year falls on a different Western date every year. (This is because the Chinese new year always falls on the second new moon after the winter solstice.) Find your birthday within the time periods indicated, and write down your element and animal sign. For example, if you were born between January 27th, 1971, and February 14th, 1972, you were born in the Chinese year of the Metal Pig.

Yearly Elements and Animal Signs

Year	Element	Animal
1/23/28–2/9/29	Earth	Dragon
2/10/29–1/29/30	Earth	Snake
1/30/30–2/16/31	Metal	Horse
2/17/31–2/5/32	Metal	Sheep
2/6/32–1/25/33	Water	Monkey
1/26/33–2/13/34	Water	Rooster
2/14/34–2/3/35	Wood	Dog
2/4/35–1/23/36	Wood	Pig
1/24/36–2/10/37	Fire	Rat
2/11/37–1/30/38	Fire	Ox
1/31/38–2/18/39	Earth	Tiger
2/19/39–2/7/40	Earth	Rabbit
2/8/40–1/26/41	Metal	Dragon
1/27/41–2/14/42	Metal	Snake

Year	Element	Animal
2/15/42–2/4/43	Water	Horse
2/5/43–1/24/44	Water	Sheep
1/25/44–2/12/45	Wood	Monkey
2/13/45–2/1/46	Wood	Rooster
2/2/46–1/21/47	Fire	Dog
1/22/47–2/9/48	Fire	Pig
2/10/48–1/28/49	Earth	Rat
1/29/49–2/16/50	Earth	Ox
2/17/50–2/5/51	Metal	Tiger
2/6/51–1/26/52	Metal	Rabbit
1/27/52–2/13/53	Water	Dragon
2/14/53–2/2/54	Water	Snake
2/3/54–1/23/55	Wood	Horse
1/24/55–2/11/56	Wood	Sheep
2/12/56–1/30/57	Fire	Monkey
1/31/57–2/17/58	Fire	Rooster
2/18/58–2/7/59	Earth	Dog
2/8/59–1/27/60	Earth	Pig
1/28/60–2/14/61	Metal	Rat
2/15/61–2/4/62	Metal	Ox
2/5/62–1/24/63	Water	Tiger
1/25/63–2/12/64	Water	Rabbit
2/13/64–2/1/65	Wood	Dragon
2/2/65–1/20/66	Wood	Snake
1/21/66–2/8/67	Fire	Horse
2/9/67–1/29/68	Fire	Sheep
1/30/68–2/16/69	Earth	Monkey
2/17/69–2/5/70	Earth	Rooster
2/6/70–1/26/71	Metal	Dog
1/27/71–2/14/72	Metal	Pig
2/15/72–2/2/73	Water	Rat
2/3/73–1/22/74	Water	Ox
1/23/74–2/10/75	Wood	Tiger
2/11/75–1/30/76	Wood	Rabbit
1/31/76–2/17/77	Fire	Dragon

Year	Element	Animal
2/18/77–2/6/78	Fire	Snake
2/7/78–1/27/79	Earth	Horse
1/28/79–2/15/80	Earth	Sheep
2/16/80–2/4/81	Metal	Monkey
2/5/81–1/24/82	Metal	Rooster
1/25/82–2/12/83	Water	Dog
2/13/83–2/1/84	Water	Pig
2/2/84–2/19/85	Wood	Rat
2/20/85–2/8/86	Wood	Ox
2/9/86–1/28/87	Fire	Tiger
1/29/87–2/16/88	Fire	Rabbit
2/17/88–2/5/89	Earth	Dragon
2/6/89–1/26/90	Earth	Snake
1/27/90–2/14/91	Metal	Horse
2/15/91–2/3/92	Metal	Sheep
2/4/92–1/22/93	Water	Monkey
1/23/93–2/9/94	Water	Rooster
2/10/94–1/30/95	Wood	Dog
1/31/95–2/18/96	Wood	Pig
2/19/96–2/6/97	Fire	Rat
2/7/97–1/27/98	Fire	Ox
1/28/98–2/15/99	Earth	Tiger
2/16/99–2/4/00	Earth	Rabbit
2/5/00–1/23/01	Metal	Dragon
1/24/01–2/11/02	Metal	Snake
2/12/02–1/31/03	Water	Horse
2/1/03–1/21/04	Water	Sheep
1/22/04–2/8/05	Wood	Monkey
2/9/05–1/28/06	Wood	Rooster
1/29/06–2/17/07	Fire	Dog
2/18/07–2/6/08	Fire	Pig
2/7/08–1/25/09	Earth	Rat
1/26/09–2/13/10	Earth	Ox
2/14/10–2/2/11	Metal	Tiger
2/3/11–1/22/12	Metal	Rabbit

Year	Element	Animal
1/23/12–2/9/13	Water	Dragon
2/10/13–1/30/14	Water	Snake
1/31/14–2/18/15	Wood	Horse
2/19/15–2/7/16	Wood	Sheep
2/8/16–1/27/17	Fire	Monkey
1/28/17–2/15/18	Fire	Rooster
2/16/18–2/4/19	Earth	Dog

Finding the Element and Animal Sign of Your Day of Birth

Since you calculated the element of your day of birth in Chapter 4, calling it your personal element, just make a note of it here and use the following method.

The way to calculate the animal sign of your day of birth is very similar to the way you calculated the element of your day of birth. For this calculation, however, use the table of animal signs and the wheel of animal signs on the following pages. The table of animal signs contains the signs for January 1st of the years 1929 to 2019. Each leap year is marked by an asterisk (*). The wheel of animal signs contains the twelve signs in clockwise order.

1. In the table, note the animal sign for January 1st of the year you were born and mark its corresponding position on the wheel.
2. Count the number of days from and including January 1st up to and including the day of your birth. Here are the number of days for each month:

January = 31	July = 31
February = 28 (29 in leap year)	August = 31
March = 31	September = 30
April = 30	October = 31
May = 31	November = 30
June = 30	December = 31

3. Divide the number you obtained in step 2 by 12.

4. Discard the quotient and keep the remainder. Note, the remainder can be any number from 0 to 11.

5. Take your remainder to the wheel and, beginning at your marked position, count clockwise as many signs as your remainder indicates. Remember, your marked position counts as position 1.

   If your remainder is 1, the animal sign of your day of birth is the same as that of your marked position. If your remainder is 0, however, count counter-clockwise one step from your marked position to find your animal sign.

Animal Signs

January 1st	Animal Sign
1929	Horse
1930	Pig
1931	Dragon
1932*	Rooster
1933	Rabbit
1934	Monkey
1935	Ox
1936*	Horse
1937	Rat
1938	Snake
1939	Dog
1940*	Rabbit
1941	Rooster
1942	Tiger
1943	Sheep
1944*	Rat
1945	Horse
1946	Pig
1947	Dragon
1948*	Rooster
1949	Rabbit

January 1st	Animal Sign
1950	Monkey
1951	Ox
1952*	Horse
1953	Rat
1954	Snake
1955	Dog
1956*	Rabbit
1957	Rooster
1958	Tiger
1959	Sheep
1960*	Rat
1961	Horse
1962	Pig
1963	Dragon
1964*	Rooster
1965	Rabbit
1966	Monkey
1967	Ox
1968*	Horse
1969	Rat
1970	Snake
1971	Dog
1972*	Rabbit
1973	Rooster
1974	Tiger
1975	Sheep
1976*	Rat
1977	Horse
1978	Pig
1979	Dragon
1980*	Rooster
1981	Rabbit
1982	Monkey
1983	Ox
1984*	Horse

January 1st	Animal Sign
1985	Rat
1986	Snake
1987	Dog
1988*	Rabbit
1989	Rooster
1990	Tiger
1991	Sheep
1992*	Rat
1993	Horse
1994	Pig
1995	Dragon
1996*	Rooster
1997	Rabbit
1998	Monkey
1999	Ox
2000*	Horse
2001	Rat
2002	Snake
2003	Dog
2004*	Rabbit
2005	Rooster
2006	Tiger
2007	Sheep
2008*	Rat
2009	Horse
2010	Pig
2011	Dragon
2012*	Rooster
2013	Rabbit
2014	Monkey
2015	Ox
2016*	Horse
2017	Rat
2018	Snake
2019	Dog

The Wheel of Animal Signs

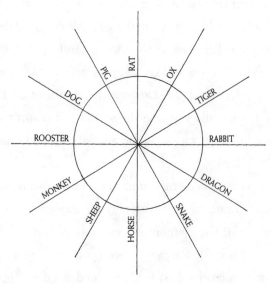

Here are three examples to demonstrate the method.

- Let's say that you were born on April 18th, 1965. First, we note that the animal sign for January 1st, 1965, is Rabbit, then mark Rabbit on the wheel of animal signs. Next, since there are 31 days is January, 28 days in February, 31 days in March, and 18 days in April up to and including the 18th, we add these to get 108. Next, we divide 108 by 12 to get 9 with 0 left over. Discarding the quotient of 9 and keeping the remainder of 0, we bring the 0 to the wheel and count counterclockwise, 1 sign from the marked position, to find that the animal sign of your day of birth is Tiger.

- To find the animal sign of the day of birth of John, born July 19th, 1972, we first note that the animal sign for January 1st, 1972, is Rabbit, then mark Rabbit on the wheel of animal signs. Next, since there are 31 days in January, 29 days in February (1972 being a leap year), 31 days in March, 30 days in April, 31 days in May, 30 days in June, and 19 days in July up to and including the 19th, we add these up to get 201. Next, we divide 201 by 12 and get 16 with 9 left over. Discarding the quotient of 16 and keeping the remainder of 9, we bring the 9 to the wheel and count clockwise 9 signs, beginning with the marked Rabbit, to find that Pig is the animal sign of John's day of birth.

▪ To find the animal sign of the day of birth of Louise, born on April 7th, 1961, we note first that the animal sign for January 1st, 1961, is Horse, then mark Horse on the wheel of animal signs. Next, since there are 31 days in January, 28 days in February, 31 days in March, and 7 days in April up to and including the 7th, we add these up to get 97. Next, we divide 97 by 12 to get 8 with 1 left over. Discarding the quotient of 8 and keeping the remainder of 1, we bring the 1 to the wheel and count the marked position as 1. Thus, we find that Horse is the animal sign of Louise's day of birth.

When you have ascertained the animal sign of your day of birth, combine it with your personal element, or element of your day of birth, as determined in Chapter 4. For example, if the element of your day of birth is Wood and the animal sign of your day of birth is Rat, you were born on the day of Wood Rat.

In the following paragraphs, first find and read the description of the element and animal sign for your year of birth. Then find and read the description of the element and animal sign for your day of birth. Try to get a sense of how the two descriptions relate to and combine with each other. Is there a marked difference between them, or are they similar? Remember, give the stronger emphasis to the element and animal sign of your day of birth.

Wood Rat

A faithful and trustworthy member of the predictably unpredictable Rat family, you are a romantic yet independent character who makes quite an adventure of courtship. You can be surprising in your seemingly impulsive advances and are even more surprising in your sexual appetite, which thrives on fantasy and an atmosphere of intrigue and daring. Not that this is meant to give anyone the impression that you are an easy catch; indeed, you are highly selective about your mate. You have quite a nose for finding what you want and will let nothing get in your way of having it. You are skillful at hatching amorous plots and can be extremely disarming in the way you display your affections. Be that as it may, you also can be surprisingly blunt toward those you find undesirable or unacceptable.

You are naturally energetic and enterprising, and have the capacity to earn a lot of money. You are also inclined to spend a lot, especially on loved ones. When you settle down, you are generally faithful, even amid the tempting variety life seems to bring your way.

Because you thrive in an orderly environment, arrange your home so that it is uncluttered, simple, and easy to move around in. It should include a special place for a library with room for your computer and other electronic equipment.

Fire Rat

If anyone in the Rat family can sell ice to the Eskimos, it surely is you. With bold declarations and a tempting manner, you are easily capable of overwhelming just about anyone who becomes the object of your desire. Like other members of the Rat family, you are extraordinarily clever at figuring out how to get whatever you want. In other words, you are an opportunist. But then what self-respecting Rat isn't? Your opportunism has two sides. On the one hand, you can easily lead others to believe things that simply aren't true by concealing your real intentions behind wonderfully enticing words and gestures. On the other hand, when you finally get serious about forming a lasting relationship, you will take advantage of every opportunity you have to do just that. You are an adventurous character. You love the chase. You also love to be in social situations where you shine and attract attention.

In love you are ardent and often jealous. Give your loved one plenty of time to get to know you: your ways are lightning fast at times and can be full of unexpected and perplexing turns.

Because you thrive in a calm environment, paradox that you are, arrange your home so that you have a private area or room where you can relax and meditate.

Earth Rat

A practical, cautious, and acquisitive character, you are less apt to make sudden moves than the other members of the Rat family. But seeing how a Rat is a Rat, you can't help but be a surprise, especially to the one you love most and for whom you gladly make sacrifices. Because you can spend so much of your time and energy working to provide secure conditions for the future, you can bewilder your loved one by your absence. However, if you were to come to see how the security of your relationship depends just as much on how happy you are together day by day as it does on paying the bills, your penchant for hard work might bring you around to working on your relationship as well.

Actually, you are a warmhearted and generous soul who would like nothing better than to have a happy home and family. It would be ideal if you and your mate were of like minds and were able to work alongside each other, or if your mate were to take a positive and supportive interest in the work you do.

Because you thrive in a joyous environment, make your home a cheerful place where you can entertain. Decorate it with warm colors, and fill it with beautiful furniture, rugs, works of art, and flowers.

Metal Rat

A most acquisitive member of the Rat family, you are clever and ingenious, and have the ability to seduce just about anyone you want. While you appear to be easygoing and nonchalant, you are really headstrong and will go your merry if precipitous way, regardless of what others say or what befalls you. Because you have a taste for challenges and risks, you are apt to cut a sharp path full of thrilling ups and downs, and end up, for better or worse, far from where you started out. While you can be sure that you will always have opportunities to find love along the way, few people will be able to keep pace with you or hold your attention long enough to become truly intimate with you. Because your attention is usually taken up by whatever is current, you can be off and running in the most unpredictable directions and leave others completely nonplussed. Not that you aren't a good lover. You are actually a great lover, that is, when you want to be. And toward that end you can be unbelievably sweet.

Because you thrive in a nurturing environment, decorate your home with warm colors and comfortable furniture, and provide it with a roomy and well-appointed kitchen. You have a talent for cooking.

Water Rat

A most engaging member of the Rat family, you are gifted with a vivid imagination and natural ability to inspire love and affection. Combining the sweet yet irresistible force of Water with the Rat's penchant for surprise, you can be a disarming flirt and charmer. You can fascinate others by your conversation, which is often spiced by your ridiculous sense of humor. You have the psychic ability to sense other people's motives and predict their moves, which you can use to your advantage.

Trust your intuition when choosing a partner. When in love, you are inclined to be lavish in affection. Nevertheless, because you are capable of giving complete devotion and fidelity, you need the same from your partner if you are to become seriously involved.

Because you thrive in an intellectual environment, arrange your home so that it contains a fine library where you can relax and enjoy your books, videos, and CDs.

Wood Ox

Unlike the more stolid members of the Ox family, you are a many-sided, if not puzzling character. You tend to spend long periods of time ruminating, calmly weighing the odds, and changing your mind again and again. While this idiosyncrasy sometimes leads others to believe you are muddleheaded, that is the furthest thing from the truth. You have a natural instinct for organization and are capable of handling all sorts of complexities.

Your taste for hard work and slow, steady progress make it important for you to live a settled life and stick to routines. While you know that this is the formula for lasting success, it might make you appear uninteresting to prospective lovers who are out for the sort of excitement and adventure that simply don't appeal to you. If you have been disappointed or offended by such people, be true to yourself. Choose someone who can appreciate you for who you are. Behind that cool, reserved air of yours, you are romantic and sexually passionate.

Because you thrive in an orderly environment, arrange your home so that it is uncluttered, simple, and easy to move around in. It should include a special place for a library with room for your computer and other electronic equipment.

Fire Ox

The most playful member of the Ox family, you are a romantic character who approaches love with all the determination and perseverance that have won the Ox the reputation of being the most reliable creature in the Chinese zodiac. With all your fire the object of your desires may safely look forward to being overwhelmed with loving attention. Indeed, once you get going there's no stopping you. Not that you are a show-off. Like all Oxen, you tend to be shy or reticent in company and develop your relationships cautiously. However, when you really love someone, you'll throw caution to the wind and express yourself openly and sincerely.

While your idea of having a good time may not be exactly the same as that of some of the more dynamic members of the zodiac, you have a great capacity for physical pleasures and enjoy, among other things, cooking, gardening, and similar joys of country life. Typical of Oxen, you also enjoy working hard and making money to provide for a comfortable home and happy family life.

Because you thrive in a calm environment, arrange your home so that you have a private area or room where you can relax and meditate.

Earth Ox

If anyone is more solid and steadfast than all the other Oxen, it surely is you, whose sign stands for everything down to earth. While you are not exactly the flamboyant type, you do have the sort of magnetism that, when combined with your proverbial patience and plodding perseverance, makes it possible for you to attract and attain just about anything you desire. You can easily win the trust of others with your sincere manner and reliability.

Because you are capable of working tirelessly and shouldering great responsibilities, you are almost certain to attain a high position that will afford the means you need to have a comfortable home and happy family life. There are those who might think you are not particularly romantic, considering your need for order and established routines. But little do they know; you are capable of a most profound and constant love that only grows richer and deeper with the years.

Because you thrive in a joyous environment, make your home a cheerful place where you can entertain. Decorate it with warm colors, and fill it with beautiful furniture, rugs, works of art, and flowers.

Metal Ox

The combination of Metal with your sign makes you the most companionable member of the Ox family. While you are not as outgoing, changeable, and quick as some of the other signs, you have a way of attracting interesting people. Your affectionate and caring attributes, combined with your sensitivity and refined ways, make others comfortable and happy in your presence.

Because you characteristically begin a love relationship in friendship, you are most likely to meet your better half through your circle of intimate friends. Considering how self-protective and inflexible you can be, you do not build your relationships lightly. Love develops slowly for you, but it becomes very deep. You are capable of becoming profoundly devoted and have little trouble making lasting commitments to the one you love. Like all Oxen, you are drawn to the joys of home and family life, and will work hard to have them.

Because you thrive in a nurturing environment, decorate your home with warm colors and comfortable furniture, and provide it with a roomy and well-appointed kitchen. You have a talent for cooking.

Water Ox

Of all the members of the Ox family, you are the sweetest and most gentle. It seems that you can take the troubles of others to heart and sacrifice yourself for them. While this is certainly beyond praise, you need to be careful not to confuse your empathic tendency with your passive tendency and let others take unfair advantage of your good nature. There seem to be no bounds to your capacity to care and feel for others. Ironically, however, when you are sexually attracted to someone, you find it hard to express your feelings.

As with all Oxen, you yearn for a loving mate who can fathom the depth of your feelings. You need someone who shares your wishes for a comfortable home and happy family, and who is willing to work with you to make those wishes come true.

Because you thrive in an intellectual environment, arrange your home so that it contains a fine library where you can relax and enjoy your books, videos, and CDs.

Wood Tiger

While all Tigers are innately intellectual, you are most noticeably so. Your insatiable curiosity and gregarious nature readily bring you into contact with all sorts of people, whose ideas and opinions are an endless source of amusement for you.

As a result, you are capable of turning yourself into a walking encyclopedia, or lying encyclopedia as the case may be, which makes you a most interesting and original conversationalist and lover. You are a true lover of life who would like nothing better than to travel down every road there is in an endless quest for experience. You are just as capable of scholarship and exploring inner space as you are of traveling across the world and exploring outer space.

The ideal mate for you is someone who shares your love of adventure and delights in your sense of humor, even your practical jokes. You are tender and indulgent as a lover, and, true to your intellectual disposition, approach lovemaking in an imaginative and playful way.

Because you thrive in a calm environment, arrange your home so that you have a private area or room where you can relax and meditate.

Fire Tiger

A most creative individual, you are passionate about whatever you do and are capable of attaining great success in life. If it is a love relationship you want, you can be sure that it, too, will be a success unless, of course, your sweetheart can't accept the imperious attitude you are apt to assume or the way your passions can run away with you. The worst thing for your sweetheart to do is show signs of possessiveness and jealousy. Where your freedom is resented or challenged, you lose patience. However, if your sweetheart has a sense of humor and ability to understand your single-minded ways and aggressive style, your relationship will be a joy. You can be a wildly imaginative lover and great fun to be with.

Because you thrive in a joyous environment, make your home a cheerful place where you can entertain. Decorate it with warm colors, and fill it with beautiful furniture, rugs, works of art, and flowers.

Earth Tiger

The combination of the element Earth with your animal sign makes you a most practical yet surprisingly inventive sort of Tiger. While you display such Tigerlike characteristics as curiosity, intellectuality, imagination, spontaneity, independence, adventurousness, and humor, you are more inclined to settle contentedly into an enduring relationship than some other members of the Tiger family. This, however, is not meant to imply that you're an easy catch. If you feel unduly pressured, you will instinctively assert your independence, even if it means breaking off your relationship. Unless you are left completely free to make your own moves in your own time, you won't settle into anything. If your partner is self-confident and supportive, however, you will naturally express your freedom by developing a lasting and joyful relationship.

Because you thrive in a nurturing environment, decorate your home with warm colors and comfortable furniture, and provide it with a roomy and well-appointed kitchen. You have a talent for cooking.

Metal Tiger

Like all Tigers, you are intellectually detached and have the ability to see different sides of an issue with equanimity. But you are the most persuasive. With the proverbial curiosity of the cat, you can engage anyone in conversation. Because you excel in small talk, some might believe you shallow, but this is far from the truth. You are actually a deep thinker and have the knack of getting to the heart of things in most paradoxical ways. While appearing to be indifferent and casual, you can trick others into coming around to your secretly held point of view as though it were their own. How nicely this works for you when you have amorous adventure in mind.

Because your ideals and interests are often unusual and far-ranging, you get along best with those who are artistic and intellectual, and whose ideas interest and amuse you.

Because you thrive in an intellectual environment, arrange your home so that it contains a fine library where you can keep your books, videos, and CDs.

Water Tiger

While you might appear to be, or wish to be, a simple, easygoing, free spirit, you are actually very complex. On the one hand, you can be cool and detached, even enigmatic. On the other hand, you are capable of showing the warmest and most tenderhearted emotions. A visionary and dreamer, you can be the angel of mercy one day and an uncompromising perfectionist the next. You are an idealist who approaches life and love like an artist and philosopher.

You give everyone and everything its proper place in an all-encompassing system of values, and in this system, it is your independence that comes first. Paradoxical as this sounds, it in no way implies that you are not a wonderful lover. Of all the members of the Tiger family, you are the most caring. Love, for you, is very much a matter of communication on many levels, not the least of which is psychic.

Because you thrive in an orderly environment, arrange your home so that it is uncluttered, simple, and easy to move around in. It should include a special place for a library with room for your computer and other electronic equipment.

Wood Rabbit

While it is true that you are hard on yourself and easy on others, the question of how faithful you are in love depends very much on how others treat you. Because you are extremely sensitive and often insecure, you can be easily confused and inclined to wander. Not that you are shallow in love. It is just that your loving and empathic proclivities are so similar that you can easily mistake one for the other and naively give yourself in love to someone who is incapable of affection. If you fail to come to terms with this and let it happen over and over again, your love life will eventually become a truly sad affair. If, however, you discriminate between your inclinations and find a suitable outlet for your empathic and altruistic proclivities, possibly joining a humanitarian or charitable organization, you will be able to set a wonderful example and associate with like-minded people, among whom you may find someone who can truly love you as you deserve to be loved.

Because you thrive in a calm environment, arrange your home so that you have a private area or room where you can relax and meditate.

Fire Rabbit

You are the most dynamic member of the Rabbit family. With your warm heart and pronounced sense of practicality, it is not uncommon for you to go out of your way to help and support others, especially those you care for. Nonetheless, your adaptable and sympathetic nature, coupled with your inclination to luxuriate in sex, can make you susceptible to being taken advantage of. While it is true that you are sensual and love physical contact, you are a romantic—your passions come from your heart. Because you need romance, you should settle for nothing less. It is precisely because you are so caring that you can attain what you want. Be good to yourself, therefore, and go out of your way to find it, if necessary.

Because you thrive in a joyous environment, make your home a cheerful place where you can entertain. Decorate it with warm colors, and fill it with beautiful furniture, rugs, works of art, and flowers.

Earth Rabbit

A genuine paragon of virtue, you are the most self-sacrificing and kindhearted sign in the Chinese zodiac. You are always well-meaning. Nonetheless, you make it nearly impossible for others to fathom you, especially when their curiosity causes you to feel at all uncomfortable. You are emotionally extremely vulnerable and apt to conceal your true feelings in an attitude of humility and bashfulness that can quite literally put others to shame. Not that your humility is feigned. You are extremely peace-loving and gentle. But it is your dread of confrontation that makes you evasive, and your evasiveness is your undoing. It can cause you to run down a labyrinth of compromising that ends in a sea of troubles, while all you really want is to be loved. You would get along best, therefore, with a partner who is just as tender as you and who doesn't try to probe or manipulate you but who delights in your attentions and shares your love of home and family.

Because you thrive in a nurturing environment, decorate your home with warm colors and comfortable furniture, and provide it with a roomy and well-appointed kitchen. You have a talent for cooking.

Metal Rabbit

The strength that sets you apart from all the other Rabbits is your superior discernment. Not only are you intuitively sensitive to others but you can understand them objectively. This ability makes you both a subtle counselor to your friends and loved ones and an excellent strategist in the world of business as well as love.

You are an artist of life and love. Your senses and tastes are often highly developed and refined. You are an aesthete who has a boundless capacity to express affection. You require constancy and closeness to open up; however, once you make a commitment you keep it. The best partner for you, therefore, is someone you can trust completely.

Because you thrive in an intellectual environment, arrange your home so that it contains a fine library where you can relax and enjoy your books, videos, and CDs.

Water Rabbit

Of all Rabbits you are the most profoundly emotional and elusive. Not that you want others to misunderstand you, but because of the depth and subtlety of your emotional nature, which even you might not fathom, you can make the most baffling moves, which leave your admirers and would-be lovers perfectly nonplussed. What lies at the bottom of this puzzling behavior is your degree of happiness. If you are essentially happy, your emotional currents are clear and smooth. If, however, you are essentially unhappy, the opposite happens. To say that your happiness or unhappiness is the fault of others, however, is to miss the mark. Self-acceptance and self-cultivation are essential for you. It is out of your inner happiness alone that you can attract the love you want and deserve. Like all Rabbits you are extraordinarily affectionate and sensuous in lovemaking, and need a loving home and family life to feel whole.

Because you thrive in an orderly environment, arrange your home so that it is uncluttered, simple, and easy to move around in. It should include a special place for a library with room for your computer and other electronic equipment.

Wood Dragon

A bold and candid Dragon, you are something of a paradox, because, while you have no trouble showing your positive feelings and asserting yourself, you are often driven by a deep sense of insecurity. You can be counted on to establish your position and drive your point home. You always want to take the lead and be in charge, and you require your partner to see things your way right or wrong.

Because you are inclined to fight for what you want in life, you are certain to be successful.

You are best suited by a partner who yields to you and gives you a secure home environment. You are inclined to be very interested in the welfare of your family and go to great lengths to provide for them. Your capacity for work is astounding. You can become so absorbed in work, however, that your loved ones might have to go for long stretches without seeing much of you. You are a dyed-in-the-wool individualist who, besides being a fun-loving and expressive lover, must have space apart. Therefore, when arranging your home, make sure that you have a room or space for yourself alone.

Because you thrive in a joyous environment, make your home a cheerful place where you can entertain. Decorate with warm colors, and fill it with beautiful furniture, rugs, works of art, and flowers.

Fire Dragon

A totally individualistic sort of Dragon, you stand alone by necessity and by choice. You are an intensely creative spirit and are endowed with strong intuitive powers. You welcome challenges and difficulties, if only to prove your strength and intelligence. Indeed, you are not at all interested in what is easy; conquest is what you relish.

Being a natural leader, you must have a willing follower, and one who has a special way of showing you the kind of admiration that fuels your fire and inspires you to tackle ever newer challenges. You have great vision and daring, and would be most delighted with a partner who shares your bold adventures. There is never a dull moment with the likes of you.

Because you thrive in a nurturing environment, decorate your home with warm colors and comfortable furniture, and provide it with a roomy and well-appointed kitchen. You have a flare for cooking.

Earth Dragon

You have a unique ability to calculate your moves, which, if not as frequent as those of the other members of the Dragon family, are often quite surprising. You are very intelligent and instinctively know how to get whatever you want. You have a way of listening calmly to others whose opinions differ from yours and of bringing them around with infinite patience to see things your way, for, typical of all Dragons, you are a leader.

What you want is all the power and wealth to obtain a proper castle far away from the crowd. There you can live in peace and quiet, and protect your loved ones from all that you abhor. Not that you are unsociable; it is characteristic of you to have an interesting circle of friends with whom you can enjoy a rich cultural life.

Because you thrive in an intellectual environment, arrange your home so that it contains a fine library where you can relax and enjoy your books, videos, and CDs.

Metal Dragon

The most commanding, energetic, and forceful member of the Dragon family, you are determined to succeed in attaining your objectives, be they wealth, artistic success, political success, or success in love. There is nothing you love more than a challenge because it gives you the chance to experience the exhilaration of winning, and win you must. Because you are intellectually detached and resourceful in ways that border on genius, you excel at calculating your moves. You have absolute conviction in your point of view and are open to disagreement only to overcome your opposition. You uphold the highest ideals for yourself and expect others to come up to them as well.

Because you are thorough in all you do, you are perfectly trustworthy and profoundly genuine in your love. Your ability to care for and protect others is utterly superior, and your need to be loved and accepted is total.

Because you thrive in an orderly environment, arrange your home so that it is uncluttered, simple, and easy to move around in. It should include a special place for a library with room for your computer and other electronic equipment.

Water Dragon

You are a subtle, mystical, and elusive Dragon who can subliminally influence others to see things your way. You are hypnotic and charismatic, psychic and forceful. You truly believe in and uphold the finest ideals and often display gentleness, courtesy, and gallantry. Nonetheless, you are a most imaginative and often inspired type who hates to be restrained; you must have freedom to realize your dreams.

Because you are a hard worker and valiant soul, you can give your all for love. A true romantic, you often lead a rich and beautiful life. You are profoundly passionate in love and find great fulfillment in providing secure and happy conditions for your loved ones.

Because you thrive in a calm environment, arrange your home so that you have a private area or room where you can relax and meditate.

Wood Snake

A most intriguing sort of Snake, you are inclined to plot your course and plan your moves long before you take action. Little do others know, when you glide their way with your casual airs and seductive glances, how deliberate you actually are. While your manner is usually very sensual, you are anything but indiscriminate. You are actually quite single-minded and know exactly what you're up to, even if others don't.

In the same single-minded way you pursue love, you pursue your other affairs. It is not uncharacteristic of you, therefore, to ignore the needs of your loved one when your interests are turned elsewhere. Because this sort of behavior can make your sweetheart jealous, or lead him or her to believe that you either don't care or are ambivalent, you need to communicate your feelings and intentions sincerely if you don't want to lose what makes you happy. You need love like a flower needs water. You are never so happy as when you are basking in the sunshine of sensual delights. You relish, among other pleasures, delicious foods and wines, beautiful clothes, perfumes and jewelry, living in a gorgeous environment, and making love. You are most uncomfortable and discontent in a messy and unaesthetic home.

Because you thrive in a joyous environment, make your home a cheerful place where you can entertain. Decorate it with warm colors, and fill it with beautiful furniture, rugs, works of art, and flowers.

Fire Snake

Of all the members of the Snake family you are the most passionate and volatile. Generally content with yourself and comfortable with your life, you are devoted to the happiness of your loved ones and will work hard to provide them with secure conditions. You are normally peace-loving and even-tempered, unless, of course, someone treads on you. When crossed you don't hesitate to strike. You are capable of vengeful behavior and can make an implacable enemy if need be. Injuries to you are long remembered; kindness is also. For this reason you need someone who truly cares for you and knows what it means to be loyal. You are very passionate in love. Colors affect your senses strongly. How you color your home can make a world of difference to you.

Because you thrive in a nurturing environment, decorate your home with warm colors and comfortable furniture, and provide it with a roomy and well-appointed kitchen. You have a talent for cooking.

Earth Snake

You are the sort of Snake who loves to relax and bask in the warmth of the sun; you are inclined to laziness and dreaming. However, because you have innate intellectual abilities and a good memory, you can be a very interesting companion who happens to be extremely sensual as well. Your sensuality so pervades your nature that you tend to view all your relationships primarily by how they feel and are capable of deriving much pleasure from many people. This in no way is meant to imply that you are promiscuous. You are actually inclined to be extremely loyal in love and will go to great lengths to make your environment secure and your lover content. You are completely trustworthy and, although prone to lying around in a sultry sort of way, are quite capable of taking care of yourself and everyone else.

Because you thrive in an intellectual environment, arrange your home so that it contains a fine library where you can relax and enjoy your books, videos, and CDs.

Metal Snake

Discriminating and gifted with the proverbial wisdom of the serpent, you are shrewd in your approach to life. Because good social relations are essential for your sense of well-being, you are extremely sensitive to others and have the ability to influence them in the most subtle ways. You instinctively aim to have an interesting circle of friends, because it is through them that you find your true love.

You would get along best with someone who is intellectual and refined, and who can appreciate your remarkably sophisticated sensuality. Because you are always interested in ideas, you make an excellent conversationalist and can adapt to, and appreciate, many points of view. Nonetheless, it takes a lot for you to trust anyone enough to make lasting commitments. If you do make a commitment, you will not easily go back on your word. If you go far into a relationship and are betrayed, however, you will reject the offender with implacable resolve.

Because you thrive in an orderly environment, arrange your home so that it is uncluttered, simple, and easy to move around in. It should include a special place for a library with room for a computer and other electronic equipment.

Water Snake

The most psychic member of the Snake family, you have the ability to see through anything; you are extremely sensitive to, and aware of, other people's feelings and unspoken thoughts. You also have a natural inclination, and ability, to soothe others and know exactly what to do to make them happy. This is not meant to imply that you can be used against your will. Indeed, it is only by being left free and having your way that you can work your wonders.

You need to be with someone you can really trust. For when you are able to trust someone you can let go and relax, and when you relax your sensual nature blossoms. It is quite natural for you to want to luxuriate in caresses and deeply imaginative lovemaking. Love for you is all embracing. Everything in life can become romantic and sensual to you. You are capable of knowing love as a mystical experience.

Because you thrive in a calm environment, arrange your home so that you have a private area or room where you can relax and meditate.

Wood Horse

If you have a motto, it would be diversity. You can easily entertain many points of view and relate to countless people with equal interest and enthusiasm. Because you are always coming and going in your Horselike fashion, you are not likely to settle down with anyone for very long, unless it is someone who can match your imagination and exuberant ways, and give you all the freedom you need.

When you are young, which might be forever, you easily fall in love at first sight and are inclined to give your all to your sweetheart until you fall in love at first sight with the next one. It also is not impossible for you to have several lovers at the same time, and to feel that you are being absolutely loyal to each of them; you are clearly not the monogamous type. You are quite a storyteller too. You can talk your way in and out of anything. It is sheer folly for anyone even to think of throwing a noose around your neck, for that is the fastest way to lose you. When and if you finally get involved with someone who not only understands you but moves along at your speed, you can, and probably will, settle down for better or for worse, providing that you're at the steering wheel. If anyone is to be in control, it will have to be you.

Because you thrive in an orderly environment, arrange your home so that it is uncluttered, simple, and easy to move around in. It should include a special place for a library with room for your computer and other electronic equipment.

Fire Horse

Of all the signs in the Chinese zodiac, the Horse is the most dynamic, and of all the members of the Horse family, you are the most active. You are also the most paradoxical. For at the heart of your powerful sense of movement there exists a wellspring of profound calm. Calm in movement, you are charismatic, quick-minded, and so persuasive in speech that you can convince anyone of anything you believe in. You are an individualist with a highly unique sense of life that you live to the hilt.

While it is not all that easy for others to follow your freedom-loving ways, you have little trouble making friends. In approaching love it is essential for you to find someone who can also be your friend if you want the relationship to last. You are lighthearted, playful, and tender in love, and are happiest with someone who lets you have your way and is able to take off on the spur of the moment to wherever you want to go.

Because you thrive in a calm environment, arrange your home so that you have a private area or room where you can relax and meditate.

Earth Horse

Down to earth and totally fun-loving, you are more inclined to be constant in love than any other member of the Horse family. With great stamina and perseverance, you are capable of striving hard to have what you want. Your intelligence and sense of practicality make you eminently capable of solving any problem that might crop up, so nothing will interfere with your aims for long. Because of your natural inclination to be faithful in love, you are often supportive and reassuring, and will always come up with ideas and suggestions to keep life amusing through all the ups and downs you are sure to experience.

You are an imaginative lover and a warmhearted, affectionate friend, and are best off with someone who is just as fun-loving and imaginative.

Because you thrive in a joyous environment, make your home a cheerful place where you can entertain. Decorate it with warm colors, and fill it with beautiful furniture, rugs, works of art, and flowers.

Metal Horse

With nerves of steel, you can keep many irons in the fire and burn the candle at both ends without showing the slightest sign of fatigue. Because you love variety, it is natural for you to explore many roads in order to find your ultimate way in life. When you live your life to the fullest, your roads will eventually converge in an unwavering and practical direction that brings you down to earth and on to real success. But because you are an original thinker, your success is entirely up to you to define. You are intuitive and creative, and, while you have the strength and vision to see great projects through, you will always be unpredictable in some way and will never let anyone control you.

You need someone who is constant and true, and has the ability to understand and accept your diverse interests and capricious ways, which can be quite bewildering at times.

Because you thrive in a nurturing environment, decorate your home with warm colors and comfortable furniture, and provide it with a roomy and well-appointed kitchen. You have an unusual talent for cooking.

Water Horse

As water runs and tides come and go, so do you. Always attracted to what is current, you change your opinions and feelings quite spontaneously. While this mercurial disposition bewilders others and makes them think you're fickle, you are always true to yourself and are sincere and faithful in love as well. How long love lasts, of course, is another question. You fall in love easily, even spontaneously, and can be quite enraptured by it. Because your imagination is so powerful, fantasy is often a major ingredient for you. You are a romantic and mystic at heart. It is the marvelous that you seek, not only in love but in everything, and you will travel far and wide, in the world and in your mind, to find it.

The best companion for you is someone who appreciates your imaginative powers and loves to listen to your ever-changing thoughts.

Because you thrive in an intellectual environment, arrange your home so that it contains a fine library where you can relax and enjoy your books, videos, and CDs.

Wood Sheep

You are an intelligent and sensitive creature who lives in a world of ideas. You can also live in a world of dreams to escape your anxieties and fears. Because you tend to be naive and unsure of yourself, especially in earlier years, you are susceptible to being used unfairly. It would help you greatly to learn to protect yourself, therefore, by establishing clear boundaries to keep at a proper distance all except those who treat you with the loving-kindness you need. In other words, learn to distinguish between those who would love you and those who would just love to walk all over you.

Although you are a deeply romantic and caring soul, it is not easy for you to start a relationship; you tend to be somewhat shy and standoffish with people you don't know. Once a relationship gets under way, however, you warm up and become very playful and affectionate. You make a dependable and serious lover and are most willing to make and keep lasting commitments, unless, of course, you've been had by another wolf.

Because you thrive in an orderly environment, arrange your home so that it is uncluttered, simple, and easy to move around in. It should include a special place for a library with room for your computer and other electronic equipment.

Fire Sheep

You are a most cheerful, generous, and passionate soul with a profoundly quiet inner nature. The more you cultivate inner peace, the more cheerful and dynamic you appear to others. Conversely, the less you cultivate your inner nature and the more you give in to your tendency to fret, the weaker and less attractive you become. Like all Sheep you are shy and insecure, especially when facing the prospect of a new relationship; it takes a bit of doing for you to overcome your doubts and misgivings. But once you break the ice you become surprisingly playful and throw yourself in, heart and soul. You are actually very courageous and when push comes to shove will show great strength and determination. For this reason you are capable of undertaking the greatest challenges and becoming completely successful in life.

You are happiest in a relationship with someone who is just as fun-loving and capable of keeping commitments as you.

Because you thrive in a calm environment, arrange your home so that you have a private area or room where you can relax and meditate.

Earth Sheep

You are a most peaceful and compassionate soul, who is sweet no matter whom you are with. You are naturally empathic and supportive to everyone, but especially to your friends and loved ones. You are always there for them and are capable of running a tight ship. Not only can you keep your own house in order but you can keep everyone else's in order to boot. Be careful. You thoughtlessly tend to take the burdens of others upon yourself, only to be rejected and hurt in the long run. When you understand that letting others work out their own problems is the best way of caring, you will free yourself from your burden of being disappointed in love. In addition, if you consider how deeply you love the whole world, you might see how it would be a good idea for you to follow a humanitarian calling.

On a more mundane level, your industrious turn of mind is sure to help you make your home beautiful and well-thought-out. Having a beautiful and comfortable home is one of the main concerns of your life. It should be a place in which you and your loved ones feel secure and happy.

Because you thrive in a joyous environment, make your home a cheerful place where you can entertain. Decorate it with warm colors, and fill it with beautiful furniture, rugs, works of art, and flowers.

Metal Sheep

You are a delicate creature who is emotionally sensitive yet able to stand alone and remain detached. It is like you to watch what is going on discreetly before deciding to get involved. When you do get involved, however, you can be very witty and playful. You have an inventive turn of mind and sense of humor that can win you many a friend and the best that life has to offer.

Because it inspires you to work hard and make money, it is essential for your well-being to have a happy and meaningful love relationship. You are the kind who spends your earnings on what gives you pleasure, and nothing pleases you more than to make your loved one happy. The romantic way of life is what you want. Besides having a beautiful home, you need to travel to exotic places. Because you are loyal and tolerant, and aim to keep your relationship on track, you can use your fine powers of discrimination to sort out problems whenever they arise. A good partner for you is someone who not only shares your sense of beauty but is as sincere and loyal as you are.

Because you thrive in a nurturing environment, decorate your home with warm colors and comfortable furniture, and provide it with a roomy and well-appointed kitchen. You have a talent for cooking.

Water Sheep

You are the most mysterious character in the Chinese zodiac. In a figurative sense your natural habitat is the most inaccessible reaches of the highest mountains. You are a dreamer and purehearted thinker. You are easily confused by the tumult of the world and have a deep need to be understood and loved. However, it is not that easy for others to understand you. Not only do you keep much to yourself but you tend to adapt to others like a chameleon. Even though you resort to this way of adapting as a passive means of self-protection, it never works in your favor. It brings you into inappropriate situations and sets you up for abuse. The lessons for you, therefore, are to be independent, to make your own decisions, and not to compromise yourself. You are much stronger than you realize. Don't be afraid of setting your boundaries and saying no.

Paradoxically, your great strength lies in your profound mysteriousness. When you accept that your deepest and most important relationship is with that mystery from which you came, and to which you will finally return, you will find the love you want in life. You have the tendency to involve yourself with and depend on people who dominate and thwart you. This is something you need to avoid. The ideal mate for you is someone who is intelligent and gentle, and who respects and cares for you with true integrity.

Because you thrive in an intellectual environment, arrange your home so that it contains a fine library where you can relax and enjoy your books, videos, and CDs.

Wood Monkey

If ever a Monkey is full of surprise, it must be you. Out of the secret depths of your mind you can come up with amazing ideas that take you and your friends off in all sorts of interesting directions filled with fun and adventure. You are an optimist and have all the energy it takes to become successful in whatever you pursue.

Because you are gregarious, willful, and independent, you are inclined to have your way and take the lead in your relationships. With whatever means you can muster, be they flattery, enticement, logic, or humor, you can convince even the most reluctant of lovers to see things your way and do what you want. Anyone who gets involved with you is bound for a lot of excitement. You are generous, sexy, and lighthearted in love, and need to be appreciated for all the great things you can do.

Because you thrive in a calm environment, arrange your home so that you have a private area or room where you can relax and meditate.

Fire Monkey

You are by far the most fun-loving and passionate member of the Monkey family. In your exuberant love of life and constant pursuit of excitement, you can easily burn the candle at both ends and be burned out as a result. Moderation does not come naturally to you, and you generally don't care to be bothered by it. You are self-reliant, headstrong, gregarious, and charismatic. You have the gift of gab and a wild sense of humor, and can charm many people with your original ideas and sexy voice. Even so, you will let only a few come close to you.

Like all Monkeys, you generally take the lead in your relationships. You need to be adored and praised. You are possessive and will not be happy with anyone unless he or she is completely loyal. When you are happy, you lavish your sweetheart with the most tender affection and are never at a loss for new ways of expressing your love.

Because you thrive in a joyous environment, make your home a cheerful place where you can entertain. Decorate it with warm colors, and fill it with beautiful furniture, rugs, works of art, and flowers.

Earth Monkey

While all Monkeys are highly intelligent and inventive, you are the most practical and least prone to the endless chattering and scampering about that often characterize them. Because you take to thought where other Monkeys take to action, you are capable of devising ingenious schemes to save labor and buy time for enjoying yourself. You are a very gregarious and humorous character who usually has a large and entertaining circle of friends and no trouble attracting love.

Endowed with an earthy sensuality, you are exuberantly playful in love and inventive and demanding in sex. But, while you value similar qualities in your lover and are often very indulgent, you will accommodate his or her demands only to a certain point. If difficult problems come up and you become unhappy, you could embroil yourself in a maze of destructive games that could ruin your relationship in the long run. Because it is natural for you to want to play the leading role, you will save yourself a lot of trouble, and enjoy yourself more, if you make this clear at the beginning of your relationships.

Because you thrive in a nurturing environment, decorate your home with warm colors and comfortable furniture, and provide it with a roomy and well-appointed kitchen. You have a talent for cooking.

Metal Monkey

Of all members of the Monkey family, you are the most ingenious and at home on the cutting edge. You are an original thinker who is endowed with tremendous strength and ability to handle the most complex situations with the greatest of ease. You are also egotistical and commanding, and will always need to play the leading role. Even though you can make a good show of open-mindedness and flexibility, the way you see things is the way they are going to have to be. Because your interests often lie beyond personal relationships and home life, your partner definitely will have to be willing to accommodate you. You are innately intellectual and creative, and are capable of attaining high goals in life. You are inclined to be self-controlled and thorough in all you do. However, you dislike monotony, and, because you are attracted to whatever is new and challenging, it is not unlike you to precipitate radical changes that can upset the routines of your household.

The ideal partner for you is someone who is not only willing to follow you but flexible and adaptable to the changes you will surely want to make along the way, and is capable of appreciating your wide range of cultural interests and absurd sense of humor.

Because you thrive in an intellectual environment, arrange your home so that it contains a fine library where you can relax and enjoy your books, videos, and CDs.

Water Monkey

Because you are an innately reserved and mercurial type, you have the ability to be aware of the most subtle connections between things. In a worldly sense, this ability makes you shrewd and opportunistic. In an abstract sense, however, it makes it you capable of acquiring vast stores of knowledge. Because you also have psychic abilities, it is not unlike you to cultivate a lively interest in metaphysical or spiritual subjects as well.

You have something of a dual personality. On the one hand, you are quite warm and engaging. On the other hand, you can be cold and analytical. Because you can display these characteristics in rapid succession, many people find you baffling. However, those who love you and are closest to you know how tender-hearted and friendly you really are. You have a playful if mysterious way. The best companion for you is someone who appreciates and respects your many-sided personality and exploratory bent.

Because you thrive in an orderly environment, arrange your home so that it is uncluttered, simple, and easy to move around in. It should include a special place for a library with room for your computer and other electronic equipment.

Wood Rooster

Of all the members of the Rooster family, you are the most complex. Essentially a peace-loving soul, you can become so critical and fussy that you will rarely find a peaceful moment. Be that as it may, your superior managerial instinct, practicality, and insatiable curiosity in addition to bringing you financial success will surely bring you such great stores of information that you will become a walking encyclopedia and build a cozy love nest that will be second to none. Like all Roosters you tend to be anxious about your appearance. Because you love to attract attention, you can be quite a show-off. To ignore you in all your gorgeous plumage would be a terrible insult. You are a very social creature and can be quite garrulous and high-spirited.

When it comes to love, you are generally careful in your choices. You need someone who is constant and faithful, understands your emotional ups and downs, and appreciates your tenderness and healthy sexual appetite.

Because you thrive in a calm environment, arrange your home so that you have a private area or room where you can relax and meditate.

Fire Rooster

While all Roosters take appearances very seriously and are proud of their beautiful plumage, you are certainly the most flamboyant. You love attracting attention and have a special way of charming people in positions of power, who can help you up in life. You are an excellent entertainer. You are often high-spirited and fun-loving, and have a vivid imagination and refined sense of style. While you are as practical as all Roosters, you are somewhat less inclined to be fussy and critical. You have an eye for larger detail and are rather flexible and liberal, because you are more interested in relating to others than in edifying them.

You have a great capacity for love. You are also very sexual and passionate, and, like all Roosters, deeply loyal to your mate and attached to home and family.

Because you thrive in a joyous environment, make your home a cheerful place where you can entertain. Decorate it with warm colors, and fill it with beautiful furniture, rugs, works of art, and flowers.

Earth Rooster

You are an easily contented, home-loving soul who would be happiest living a quiet life. Although you love order and are inclined to be fussy at times, your peaceful nature softens your edge and lets you show your affections in a gentle, caring way, which often is expressed in how you keep your home. You are practical and handy and content to putter around. You would be happiest living with your brood in a house in the country where friends come for frequent visits. You are very social in a cozy sort of way. You most enjoy warm, intimate gatherings and make friendships that last for life. You also take deep pleasure in family life and will make great efforts to provide for everyone's comfort.

When it comes to love, you are naturally careful about choosing a mate. The best partner for you is someone who is loyal and deeply loving, and who appreciates your earthy sensuality and great capacity for pleasure.

Because you thrive in a nurturing environment, decorate your home with warm colors and comfortable furniture, and provide it with a roomy and well-appointed kitchen. You have a talent for cooking.

Metal Rooster

A practical, efficient, and loyal type, you are happiest among intellectual friends with whom you can have interesting conversations and share many cultural interests. Because you take great pride in your social connections, you are eager for the company of celebrities and persons of consequence. Typical of all Roosters, you take the way you look very seriously. You give much thought to how you groom and dress yourself. You are neat and well-organized, and love to display your elegant plumes.

Because you want to appear special and attract attention, you are careful and discriminating when looking for a mate. You nearly always approach relationships in a levelheaded way. You would be happiest with a mate who is loyal and intelligent, and who appreciates your excellent taste and refined sensuality.

Because you thrive in an intellectual environment, arrange your home so that it contains a fine library where you can relax and enjoy your books, videos, and CDs.

Water Rooster

While you are intelligent, reflective, and emotionally subtle, you are a creature of habit. Once you figure out a way of doing something, you will not change it. Typical of Roosters, you are critical and alert, and, while you are less apt to be outspoken and blunt than some of the others, you can be harshly critical in private in an indirect and sarcastic way. One wouldn't know this about you without knowing you intimately, however; you are generally discreet, easygoing, and lighthearted in public. You love company and witty conversation, and readily attract others with your sparkling sense of humor.

When it comes to finding a mate, you are cautious. You will watch someone who attracts you for a long time, then carefully calculate your moves. Because you want a relationship that endures, you form bonds slowly and tenderly. You will not be happy unless you are with someone who is loyal and caring, and whose sexual appetite is as healthy as yours.

Because you thrive in an orderly environment, arrange your home so that it is uncluttered, simple, and easy to move around in. It should include a special place for a library with room for your computer and other electronic equipment.

Wood Dog

You are an affectionate, fun-loving, and sexy character who can make friends with just about anyone. Always poking your nose into whatever catches your attention, you are easily taken up by flirtations and may have many affairs before you decide to settle down. You generally find it difficult to make decisions and commitments. In your earlier years you dislike having to be tied down, preferring to go after whatever attracts you at the moment. But this is how trouble starts for you. On the one hand, you are gregarious and want to please everyone. On the other hand, you are passionate and jealous, and if someone betrays or disappoints you you become embittered and confused, in spite of your good judgment. Eventually, your tendency to take life more seriously brings you to the decisions and commitments you need to make to be happy in love and in life.

Because you thrive in a joyous environment, make your home a cheerful place where you can entertain. Decorate it with warm colors, and fill it with beautiful furniture, rugs, works of art, and flowers.

Fire Dog

You are a warmhearted, playful, and affectionate character who is curious about everything and everyone. You are genuinely friendly, are always willing to give a helping hand, and love to get into all sorts of conversations that give you a good excuse to flirt. You are a very sexy character who is endowed with a vivid imagination and ribald sense of humor.

While you definitely want to find your one and only, you often stop along the way to get to know and play with those who come along, most of whom are not up to your speed. For this reason you can have a number of flirtations and affairs before you arrive at your goal of settling down. Typical of Dogs, you have excellent judgment but find it neither easy nor desirable to have to make up your mind about anything important. Rather, you are something of a troubleshooter who weighs all the pros and cons, and worries forever about what could go wrong in the future. Once you do make up your mind, however, you are most unlikely to change it. You are happiest with someone who, in addition to indulging your fantasies and keeping you sexually satisfied and happy, is as good a conversationalist and as much a bon vivant as you.

Because you thrive in a nurturing environment, decorate your home with warm colors and comfortable furniture, and provide it with a roomy and well-appointed kitchen. You have a talent for cooking.

Earth Dog

While Dogs in general find it difficult, worrisome, and unpleasant to make decisions, you are the exception. Because you are practical and judicious, and genuinely concerned for the happiness and well-being of others, you are honest and loyal to all you befriend. Out of a moral sense of fairness to others, you will make conscientious efforts to overcome whatever weaknesses you have and curb your more selfish impulses. To an equal degree, you will make great efforts to guide and counsel others. However, you really can take it too far. With all your moralizing and analyzing, and tendency to be serious and dogmatic, you sometimes give others the impression that you are a teacher or preacher, even though you are just advocating ideals that you believe everyone should follow. Actually, you are uncomfortable in the position of leader and would much rather be one of the pack, albeit a perfectly upstanding member of the community.

When it comes to love, you are faithful and conscientious, and will make great efforts to build a secure and happy home. You are happiest with someone who is as faithful and sociable as you, and who can keep you sexually satisfied and intellectually stimulated.

Because you thrive in an intellectual environment, arrange your home so that it contains a fine library where you can relax and enjoy your books, videos, and CDs.

Metal Dog

Of all the members of the Dog family, you are the most alert and ambitious. Possessing extraordinary self-discipline and independence, you are capable of greater good or greater ill than any other sign in the Chinese zodiac. Because you are deeply passionate and idealistic, you can devote your entire life to a mission you believe is for the good of the world. You are something of a crusader. You are a hard worker who can perform well under pressure and who has an excellent sense of detail and precision. However, you dislike humdrum routines and, because you have the ability to take tremendous risks and precipitate radical changes, you can boldly walk out of professional and personal conditions that bore or disappoint you.

You most value friendship, intelligent communication, and shared cultural and spiritual values in a relationship. The best mate for you is someone whose courage equals yours but who accepts your protectiveness and desire to lead, and who knows how to keep you sexually satisfied and intellectually refreshed while giving you the comfortable distance you often need.

Because you thrive in an orderly environment, arrange your home so that it is uncluttered, simple, and easy to move around in. It should include a special place for a library with room for your computer and other electronic equipment.

Water Dog

All Dogs are deep thinkers. However, you are the deepest of them all. You are also the most skillful at hiding what you think. You can appear nonchalant and upbeat even when you are troubled. You also can be very sociable and inclined to entertain many friendly contacts and flirtations while you are actually distrustful and insecure. This combination of gregariousness and suspicion, besides being bad for your nerves, often makes you appear confused. You are gifted with a fundamentally sound sense of judgment; however, it is difficult for you to trust it. You dislike having to make important decisions and can waste a lot of time in aimless habits of anxiety. Like the dog who repeatedly digs up old bones and sniffs around for who knows what, you find it difficult to resolve doubts. However, if you trust yourself and accept what you want in life, nothing will stand in your way of getting it.

When it comes to love, you can charm anyone with your friendly manner and sincerity. You are generous and trustworthy, romantic and deeply sensual.

Because you thrive in a calm environment, arrange your home so that you have a private area or room where you can relax and meditate.

Wood Pig

Because you are the most romantic and kindhearted member of the Pig family, it is the hardest thing in the world for you to say no, especially when you are in love. While this may bring you close to others, it makes you extremely vulnerable. In spite of your great intelligence, it is not unlike you to be seduced and betrayed or played for a fool, especially earlier in life. However, you are always capable of fighting back with savage courage.

You are generally bold in the face of challenges and, because you are inclined to work hard to attain the things you want in life, are capable of creating a warm and comfortable environment for yourself and your mate. You are extremely sensual, caring, and generous in love. However, because you need to bond with your partner, you can become jealous and possessive.

Because you thrive in a joyous environment, make your home a cheerful place where you can entertain. Decorate it with warm colors, and fill it with beautiful furniture, rugs, works of art, and flowers.

Fire Pig

While you are deeply passionate and nurturing toward those you love, your ever-changing moods and emotional extremes make it difficult for others to understand you. Nonetheless, you are a jovial and gregarious individual who is inclined to attract many pleasure-loving friends and admirers. You are an extremely luxurious and generous soul. You have very expensive tastes and can easily live beyond your means. When you love someone, you lavish him or her with affection. Because you are extremely sensuous, sympathetic, and tenderhearted, and often find it impossible to refuse anything to your loved one, you are emotionally vulnerable and prone to having your feelings hurt. Few people can begin to fathom the depth of your feelings; you love unquestioningly.

Because you thrive in a nurturing environment, decorate your home with warm colors and comfortable furniture, and provide it with a roomy and well-appointed kitchen. You have a talent for cooking.

Earth Pig

While all Pigs love the pleasures of home life, you are the most capable of working hard to build a secure and happy environment for your loved ones. You are extremely loyal and content to stay with one partner through thick and thin. You are also very tolerant and gentle, and, while your generosity and openness make you vulnerable to being taken unfair advantage of, you are capable of making extraordinary sacrifices for the sake of your relationship. The best companion for you is someone who is loyal and sincere, and who enjoys your deep sensuality while keeping you mentally stimulated.

You are naturally peaceable. You love to relax and take it all in stride. Because you have a deep love for the earth and all that is sensual, you would be happiest living in a beautiful house in the country where you could tend a garden and enjoy the simple pleasures of life.

Because you thrive in an intellectual environment, arrange your home so that it contains a fine library where you can relax and enjoy your books, videos, and CDs.

Metal Pig

While you lack none of the emotional depth and sensuality that characterize Pigs as a group, you are by far the most refined. You are characteristically jovial, pleasure-loving, and loyal to your friends. You have a deeply loving nature and find it hard to say no, but you are less apt to be taken unfair advantage of than the other Pigs because your Metal element gives you the ability to discriminate and set boundaries that keep you from harm. Like all Pigs you are a valiant fighter in the face of adversity, and, because you are altruistic, practical, and social, your fighting spirit can easily involve you in community affairs and humanitarian causes.

You tend to view life in an idealistic, often visionary way, which, although stemming from your deepest emotions, you express intellectually, even abstractly. For this reason you can express your love in the most poetic ways. You are extremely sensual and playful in love, and capable of the most surprising inspirations.

Because you thrive in an orderly environment, arrange your home so that it is uncluttered, simple, and easy to move around in. It should include a special place for a library with room for your computer and other electronic equipment.

Water Pig

An extremely sensitive and empathic creature, you are the most emotionally sensitive member of the Pig family. Because you are often unaware of the depth and complexity of your emotions, you can easily fall in love with the wrong person and be hurt deeply as a result. You tend to be possessive and to love so intensely that you can sacrifice yourself and all that you have. When you are in a bad relationship, your tendency to doubt yourself can prevent you from breaking it off, even though you, like all Pigs, are capable of protecting yourself with ferocious courage. If you let yourself be hurt it can take you years to overcome the pain. You are an extremely sensual, purehearted, and luxury-loving soul who needs someone just as jovial, supportive, and purehearted as you are.

Because you thrive in a calm environment, arrange your home so that you have a private area or room where you can relax and meditate.

Exercises

- Note the environmental suggestions at the ends of the descriptions for your year and day of birth signs. Because these suggestions have personal meaning, enter them in your Personal Data list.

- Combine or synthesize your foregoing astrological readings with all the information you have gathered about yourself from the earlier chapters to complete your astrological portrait.

Your Astrological Compatibilities

Now that you know the element and animal signs of your year and day of birth, let's see how they compare with those of your partner. The seventy-eight combinations of the twelve animal signs are described in this chapter. Find the descriptions that pertain to you and your partner. First read the description comparing the animal signs of your respective years of birth. Then read the description comparing the animal signs of your respective days of birth. Only compare your year sign to the year sign of your partner, and your day sign to the day sign of your partner. Don't compare your year sign to his or her day sign, or your day sign to his or her year sign. If you don't know your partner's actual day of birth but know how old he or she is, just compare your year signs.

After the seventy-eight comparative descriptions of the animal signs, you will find the fifteen comparative descriptions of the five elements. These descriptions qualify, or modify, the way the animal signs relate to each other; they either intensify or weaken the positive or negative effects of the animal sign combinations. For example, while Rabbit and Sheep are essentially in harmony with each other, Water Rabbit will get along more easily with Wood Sheep than with Fire Sheep, because the conflict of Water and Fire challenges the relationship. To give another example, while Rat and Rabbit are essentially in discord, Water Rat will get along more successfully with Wood Rabbit than with Fire Rabbit, because the conflict of Fire and Water intensifies the discordant relationship between Rat and Rabbit.

Your Animal Sign Compatibility

Rat and Rat

Because you have the same sign, you share many positive and negative characteristics. Much depends on how sincerely you love each other and whether you share goals. Rat can be very good-natured and gregarious. It is capable of adapting to a great variety of conditions and is generous toward its loved ones. It is also a very sensual and playful creature. On the other hand, Rat is aggressive and egotistical, and will not hesitate to take advantage of others for selfish reasons. When you are in agreement, you get along marvelously. However, when you are not in agreement, you can fight. If offended, Rat can be retaliatory.

Rat and Ox

While this might seem an unlikely combination, considering the speed of the Rat and the slowness of the Ox, it can work well, especially in a practical sense. This combination tends to bring the Rat down to earth and encourage the Ox to be productive. It is questionable, however, whether the Ox will be able to provide the Rat with the mental stimulation it seeks, unless, of course, the Rat appreciates the Ox's constructive abilities and logical approach to life. All in all, however, the strong earthiness of the Ox combined with the Rat's playful and affectionate nature can result in a deeply sensual kind of relationship.

Rat and Tiger

Whether the two of you can get along depends to a large extent on the goals you have in common and how much you are willing to accept each other's character traits. In spite of the fact that both of you are egotistical and indomitable, the Rat's ability to support the Tiger's unpredictable, even unconventional behavior can keep the relationship alive and well. However, when the Rat tries to manipulate or abuse the Tiger, or when the Tiger imperiously tries to put the Rat in its place, the proverbial cat and mouse game will surely follow. Both Rat and Tiger are adventurous and daring; arguments between them can escalate to the point of no return. On the brighter side, however, the Tiger's wild imagination combined with the Rat's sensuality can make your relationship exciting to say the least. You both are passionate and playful.

Rat and Rabbit

This is a discordant combination. How well you get along depends on how well you as individuals understand yourselves. You are both cunning but in opposite ways. The Rat schemes resourcefully, while the Rabbit sidesteps. The Rat is bold, while the Rabbit dreads being confronted. The Rat resorts to cunning as a way of getting what it wants; the Rabbit resorts to cunning as a way of escaping what it doesn't want. The Rat alarms the Rabbit; the Rabbit thwarts the Rat. While both are sensual and affectionate, the Rabbit's need for peace and quiet can bore the Rat, who would much rather go on an adventure. By contrast, the Rat's playfulness and surprising manner can make the Rabbit very apprehensive. If the Rat cares enough to give the Rabbit the mental space it needs, and if the Rabbit learns to trust the Rat, the relationship might stand a chance of working.

Rat and Dragon

Considering how egotistical you both are, one might wonder how you can get along. But you are extremely compatible. The Dragon is the more forceful of these two signs. Nonetheless, the clever Rat can easily bring the Dragon around to its way of thinking when differences arise. This is not meant to imply that the Rat can go overboard and boss the Dragon around. Indeed, the Dragon can make mincemeat of the Rat if it wants to. If the Dragon loves the Rat, however, it will provide the Rat with a cozy place to nest and play together. While the Dragon is protective and supportive, it is never dull; it shares its love of excitement with the equally adventurous Rat. The Dragon will always fight for what it wants in life, and if it wants the Rat, the Rat is in for a wonderful time.

Rat and Snake

Even though the Snake holds a great deal of erotic fascination for the Rat, it is not likely that this relationship will go far unless the Rat is willing to adapt to the Snake's leisurely ways. While both are naturally clever, the Rat can easily under-estimate the Snake. The Snake characteristically keeps its own counsel and watches everything secretly. The Rat, by contrast, is an extremely restless character who can become bored by the Snake's apparent indifference. When bored the Rat will look for a way out. But if the Rat tries to fool the Snake, the Snake will strike. The Snake is a jealous and possessive creature who is capable of vengeance if crossed. If the Rat and Snake fight, they can do a great deal of harm to each other. If you want to get along and have a successful relationship, therefore, you must respect each other and relate to each other with true integrity.

Rat and Horse

This is a challenging combination. Both of you are extremely energetic and restless types who tend to become scattered. Your attraction for each other holds the promise of adventure and excitement as well as a shared mental brilliance that could be a source of delight for both of you. Nonetheless, it may be difficult for you to remain together long. The Rat is an extremely cunning and independent character who is capable of taking deliberate advantage of others. The Horse, by contrast, while appearing to be independent, is somewhat naive and unstable, and needs to have supportive friends in order to feel powerful. While the Rat can see this in the Horse and take advantage of it, the Rat will eventually become bored and move on, especially if the Horse's interest in the Rat wavers. The success of your relationship, therefore, depends on the agreements you make and your sincerity in keeping them.

Rat and Sheep

This is a discordant combination. The only way it can work is if both of you become aware of yourselves and learn to respect your differences. While the Rat and the Sheep both have strong emotional natures, the Sheep is usually unaware of the Rat's scheming until it's too late. The Sheep is a rather naive and timid character, or so it seems, who cannot help but love with a pure and trusting heart. The Rat, of course, is a most charming and affectionate character who will make its moves whether the Sheep likes them or not. The Sheep tends to put up with just about anything if it feels the relationship has a chance. However, when the Sheep is pushed too far, it will surprise even the surprising Rat and shut the door for good. The Sheep, while peaceful, is far more independent than the excitable and sociable Rat. A relationship between these two can work if the Rat is willing ultimately to settle down to a quiet life with the rather mysterious Sheep. The Sheep tends to look upon the Rat's world as a threat, especially if the Rat is inclined to be inconstant.

Rat and Monkey

This is an excellent combination. While the two of you are egotistical and cunning, you are most positively compatible, even more so if the Monkey is supportive of the Rat. When you put your minds together, there is nothing you can't achieve. Because you both are so clever, you are experts of mutual seduction and know how to make each other feel very desirable. You are both adventurous and fun-loving, and are capable of finding endless ways of enjoying the world together. Because you are sociable and natural strategists, you can attract a large circle of friends, many of whom will help you attain professional and financial success. For this reason you can live in the best of circumstances together. The only danger in this combination is that neither of you is particularly inclined to be faithful. However, if you make commitments and keep them, your relationship stands an excellent chance of flourishing.

Rat and Rooster

How well the two of you get along depends to a great extent upon how skillfully the Rooster gives support to the wily Rat, and how much the Rat is willing to accept the Rooster's brand of support. If, however, the Rooster wants support from the Rat, it will come only when it suits the Rat to give it. The unpredictability of the Rat will cause the Rooster to feel unsettled. Conversely, the Rooster's need for regularity will not appeal to the Rat. You both are very sociable and amiable, and have big sexual appetites. However, when the softhearted Rooster complains to the Rat about its unpredictable ways, the Rat will criticize the Rooster rather more harshly. If the Rooster falls to squabbling with the Rat, the Rat will retaliate. This relationship will be difficult to keep on an even keel unless the two of you learn to respect your different character traits.

Rat and Dog

This is a very playful pair. The Rat is attracted to the Dog like a bee to honey, considering how amiable and sexy the Dog is. If the Dog likes what it sees in the Rat, it will be willing to set off on just about any adventure the Rat has in mind. Conversely, the Rat makes a great friend to the Dog and, being a daring character, will go along with just about anything the Dog wants to do. Because the two of you can be so considerate and generous to each other, you are capable of sharing a successful and happy life.

Rat and Pig

The basic difference between these two is that the Rat is perfectly content to run along the surface of life while the Pig loves to plumb its depths. The Rat is intuitive and opportunistic, while the Pig is sensitive and vulnerable. If the two of you become emotionally entangled and the Pig gets hurt, you could do much to harm each other; you both have bad tempers. How well you get along depends on how deeply the Pig understands the mercurial Rat and how much the Rat values the sensual and jovial Pig. Nonetheless, the Rat will tend to be uneasy about the Pig's emotional extremes, and the Pig will tend to withdraw suspiciously if the Rat can't answer its needs. It will take a lot of sincere communication for the two of you to explore and develop your relationship. But, considering the great capacity for love you share, your communication might prove interesting and rewarding.

Ox and Ox

Because you have the same sign, you share many positive and negative characteristics. The success of your relationship depends largely upon how well you accommodate each other. You generally refuse to make changes unless they agree with your sense of logic. If you have differences and one of you tries to coerce the other, push will inevitably come to shove and you will both throw your logic to the wind and carry on like a pair of raging bulls. Unless you learn to temper your stubbornness with liberality, loving-kindness, and compassion, you can do a lot of harm to your relationship. On a brighter note, if you care enough for each other to work through your differences, you can use your stubbornness in a more positive way; you are capable of working hard to keep your relationship strong and stable. The best thing about your willfulness is that you are absolutely faithful.

Ox and Tiger

Both of you are equally strong willed and independent. However, you have major differences, which you will have to understand and accept if you want your relationship to work. The Ox is naturally methodical, while the Tiger is unpredictable and playful. Because the down-to-earth Ox tends to be conservative and sedate, it is happy to follow routines. The unconventional Tiger, by contrast, tends to become bored by routines and prefers a more varied lifestyle. Depending on how deeply you love each other, your different temperaments will either bring you closer together or drive you apart. While you both are capable of deep love, the Ox is simpler, more restrained and constant, while the Tiger is restless, changeable, and inclined to wander if discontent. Because you both can be jealous, be careful: you have outrageous tempers.

Ox and Rabbit

This could turn out to be a most peaceful and loving relationship, in which the Ox approaches the Rabbit with all the discretion and geniality the Rabbit needs to feel secure, and the Rabbit gives the Ox all the affection it loves to receive. The solid and steady nature of the Ox allows the Rabbit to go about its life without feeling threatened. The Rabbit is a very affectionate creature who needs absolute fidelity, and this is precisely what the Ox can give. The Ox, being down to earth and having a great sense of responsibility, will work hard to provide the Rabbit with a warm and loving environment. While your relationship may not be the most thrilling, it can last for a long time and be filled with untold happiness and peace.

Ox and Dragon

The success of your relationship depends to a great extent on whether you share the same objectives and whether the Ox is willing to accept the Dragon's inevitable pressuring. The Dragon is generally the most dynamic and forceful creature in the Chinese zodiac. It is capable of tremendous creative activity. While the Dragon is protective and supportive, it is attracted by challenges and will fight passionately for what it wants in life. The Ox, by contrast, is a generally conservative and practical creature. It will always resist change. The Ox can be extremely stubborn, and, if prodded too much, can turn into a raging bull. Nonetheless, if the two of you love each other and make the necessary allowances for your character traits, the Ox can provide the Dragon with the stable environment it really needs.

Ox and Snake

Your relationship can work very well, especially if the Snake is emotionally supportive of the Ox. Because both of you are generally calm, well-grounded, and reasonable, you can build a sane and secure way of life that affords you much leisure to enjoy each other's company. While the Snake tends to be more sensual and luxury-loving than the Ox, the Ox is capable of delighting the Snake with its tenderness and sexual energy. Because both of you are inclined to be faithful and are attracted to the comforts of home life, your relationship will probably last a long time and bring you much happiness and peace.

Ox and Horse

This is a discordant combination. The only way your relationship can work is if both of you become aware of yourselves and are willing to adjust to each other's needs. Both of you are more or less independent and nonadaptive. The Horse is a boisterous character who thrives on excitement and adventure, and loves to be on the move. The Ox, by contrast, is a quiet and levelheaded character who generally hates surprises and spontaneous changes, and is perfectly content with routines. The Ox is also an absolutely faithful character and will devote itself to building up secure conditions for itself and its mate. The Horse, by contrast, is characteristically faithful as long as it doesn't lose interest; unless it has an undying interest in the Ox's ways, it is unlikely to stay around long enough to discover the depth of the Ox's love. However, if the Horse finds a variety of outlets for its abounding energies while remaining faithful, and the Ox respects the Horse's love of freedom, not only will your relationship work but it will be of great benefit to you.

Ox and Sheep

This is a difficult combination. Even though the two of you are pastoral, peaceable characters, there are profound and subtle differences between you that can frustrate your relationship unless you are willing to work creatively with them. While the Sheep is no less intelligent than the Ox, it is inclined to live more in its feelings, and is far more prone to nervousness. The Ox, by contrast, has a colder nature, and, while it has deep feelings, tends to think in practical and businesslike ways. The Sheep will come up with wonderfully imaginative ideas that the Ox will either ignore or quash unless they accord with its sense of practicality and reason. Because the Ox can be rigid and authoritarian, it can intimidate the Sheep. At worst, the Ox will think that the Sheep is an annoying fool, and the Sheep will feel hurt. When the Sheep is hurt, it walks away. The relationship can work, however, if the stubborn Ox is able to see the value of what the Sheep has to offer and if the Sheep is able to control its tendency to fret. While there certainly is the possibility of deep love, there is a potential power struggle in your relationship.

Ox and Monkey

Considering how the Ox resists pressure, and how the Monkey will force its way if necessary, it is unlikely that your relationship will work unless you make efforts to respect and accept each other's character traits. Without respect the Ox will have no reason to trust the Monkey, and the Monkey will have no reason to play fair. If trust is established, however, and the Ox finds a way to support the Monkey's aims, the Monkey will work wonders for the Ox that can only bring the two of you endless delights. Because both of you are hardworking and capable of attaining whatever you want, there is no reason to think you cannot stay together forever. Nonetheless, one might question how well the solid Ox can give the Monkey all the praise and excitement it needs to feel happy, or whether the sportive Monkey can give the Ox the peace and quiet it needs to feel content.

Ox and Rooster

This combination has excellent possibilities. Because the two of you are very orderly and attracted to the pleasures of a warm and secure home life, your relationship is apt to be peaceful and productive, especially if the Ox is emotionally supportive of the Rooster. While both of you are naturally intelligent, you have some differences that can make your relationship rather interesting. The Ox is a quiet and down-to-earth sort of creature who is inclined to think practically and logically. The Rooster, by contrast, is an inquisitive character who is alert, critical, and gifted with an artistic flare. It also is loquacious and witty. Because of these differences, the Rooster can make the sullen Ox feel cheerful, and the Ox can make the Rooster feel secure and cared for. Your relationship, while peaceful and quiet, will also have an element of deep passion. There is one thing you have in common: you both have big sexual appetites.

Ox and Dog

This is a difficult combination, especially for the Dog. Not that you can't get along, but it will take a bit of hard work. Fortunately, the two of you are hard workers and if you love each other can stay together through thick and thin despite your differences. The Dog has a more complicated nature than the Ox. It tends to be fretful. Because it is doubting and analytical, and instinctively looks for what's wrong in everything, it can take a long time to come to decisions. It seeks alternatives every step of the way. The Ox, by contrast, is stolid. Its aims are invariable. Because it never questions what it instinctively knows to be right, it just marches on, come what may. This intrepidity can unnerve the Dog. If the Dog accepts where the Ox is going and generates positive faith, however, it should have no reason to fret. It will not find a more faithful and loving companion anywhere than the Ox.

Ox and Pig

This combination has some wonderful possibilities, considering how deeply sensual and faithful you both are. While the Ox can look upon the Pig as a great friend, the Pig will probably be very content to let the Ox arrange all the plans and details. Not that the Pig is lazy, the Pig is actually hardworking. But to please the Ox the jovial Pig will let it do what it does best. The Ox is a great organizer and is very responsible. Your only danger is your stubbornness. While your love can overrule any differences you might have, you both can be obstinate and opinionated. You could reach an impasse in your relationship if you disagree with each other's intentions and are unwilling to work through them.

Tiger and Tiger

Because you have the same sign, you share many positive and negative characteristics. To say the least, a relationship between two Tigers is bound to be filled with surprises. You both are restless and unpredictable, and inclined to go to emotional extremes. You also tend to be jealous and not always faithful, and can become enraged if offended. The Tiger is an independent creature. It also is unconventional and intellectual. Because you are gifted with a wild imagination and sense of humor, your potential for erotic fantasy is beyond anyone's ability to describe. The success of your relationship depends on how much interest you hold for each other.

Tiger and Rabbit

What a dainty morsel the Rabbit is for the Tiger. If this relationship seems a bit out of balance, that's because it is! To begin with, the Rabbit's tendency to hide its true feelings will do nothing but titillate the Tiger's insatiable curiosity, while the Tiger's curiosity will do nothing but persuade the Rabbit to run and hide as best as it can. If the Tiger plays its cards right, however, it might get the Rabbit to come out and play. Surely the potential for much love is there. The Tiger's humor and spontaneity can easily bring out the more whimsical and imaginative side of the Rabbit. The Rabbit has more than enough erotic energy to satisfy even the wildest of Tigers. The only area where trouble really can develop is the Rabbit's possessiveness. If the Rabbit, out of insecurity, demands absolute fidelity of the Tiger, the Tiger will probably run away out of boredom. The Tiger is an independent creature who won't willingly put up with restraints. The best way for the Rabbit to keep the Tiger, therefore, is to let the Tiger be.

Tiger and Dragon

While you have equally creative and destructive possibilities, this relationship stands the best chance of working if the Tiger accepts the Dragon as its friend, and the Dragon accepts the Tiger's challenge as an invitation to attain the highest goals. While both of you are passionate, proud, unpredictable, and daring, the Dragon will force its way while the Tiger will gain the day by sheer mental brilliance. If you cooperate, you will rise to great success. If you clash, however, you will raise the roof. Both of you are quick tempered and fierce, and will fight to have your way, even to the point of ruining all the good things you share. If you weather your inevitable storms, however, your love will only deepen.

Tiger and Snake

This is a discordant combination. Your relationship might work, however, if the Tiger chooses to be emotionally supportive of the Snake, and the Snake accepts the Tiger's detached ways. On the one hand, if the Tiger is not so supportive but fools around, as it is apt to do, the astute Snake will wait for its best moment to strike. The Tiger would be making a big mistake by underestimating the Snake's intelligence. If the Snake, on the other hand, expects the Tiger to behave like another Snake, it will be unpleasantly surprised. While the quiet and sensual Snake loves to bask in the sun, the restless and daring Tiger loves to hunt. The Snake has a hypnotic way of attracting what it wants. However, it cannot rivet the Tiger's attention forever. The Tiger becomes bored by monotony. The main difference between you is that you move at different speeds, in different rhythms. If you can accept your differences, there is no reason why your relationship can't work; you both have a great love of pleasure.

Tiger and Horse

This is an excellent combination. You share much that will make your relationship a joy, to say the least, especially if the Tiger gives emotional support to the Horse. Because you probably fell in love quite suddenly, if not at first sight, there is little cautioning that either of you will care to listen to. You are both extremely freedom-loving and adventurous, and have much ability to understand each other. There is almost nothing you cannot accomplish together. You are exuberant and passionate, and can be quite eloquent when expressing your feelings to each other. And because you both are gifted with imagination and humor, your potential for erotic fantasy is phenomenal.

Tiger and Sheep

If ever there was an odd couple, you're it! Not that your relationship can't work. It can, especially if the Tiger thinks of the Sheep more as its friend than as a tasty morsel. Nevertheless, it would help the Sheep to view the Tiger as a challenge. In other words, the Sheep would do well, especially in the earlier stages of this relationship, to keep its eyes open, because in its instinctive wish to be protected it becomes vulnerable to being used. Or, as Shakespeare put it, "When the lion fawns upon the lamb, the lamb will never cease to follow him." The Sheep is generally a quiet creature, content to keep to its beaten track. Except for an occasional journey, the Sheep is very attached to its home. While there must be some Tigers who would be happy to live in peace with the imaginative, dreamy Sheep, the Tiger is normally a restless creature whose feelings can change unpredictably. Your differences notwithstanding, your relationship can work if you agree to be faithful to each other and to honor your respective needs for space. Because you both have a great deal of creative ability, your life together can be rich and productive.

Tiger and Monkey

This is a difficult combination. While the two of you certainly are fun-loving, you also love giving orders and hate to obey. It is only a matter of time before you clash. If you want your relationship to work, the Monkey will have to exercise discretion and treat the Tiger as its friend, and the Tiger will have to make the best of the Monkey's well-meaning challenges. The Monkey is a fascinating and sexy character. It is also headstrong and cunning, and apt to force its way on others. The Tiger, by contrast, is extremely independent and unpredictable, and is apt to become enraged if offended. If a disagreement arises between you, you could use anything as an excuse for fighting. However, if you develop a sincere friendship, there is no limit to the good things you can share. The two of you are very imaginative and humorous, and insatiably curious. If it is about each other that you are curious, there is literally no end to what you will discover.

Tiger and Rooster

This is a rather unlikely combination. Considering how different you are, it may be difficult for you to understand and be at peace with each other. In a nutshell, the Rooster loves consistency and the Tiger loves surprises. The Rooster is a practical creature who can be obsessive over details. The Tiger, by contrast, is an imaginative and artistic character. It is bold and unconventional, and is quickly bored by monotony. The Rooster is generally comfortable in a small and well-organized environment. The Tiger, however, is not comfortable unless it has vast spaces in which to roam freely. While the Tiger's roving instinct causes the Rooster to feel anxious, the Rooster's nesting instinct causes the Tiger to feel uncomfortable. Nonetheless, because you both are intelligent and generally outspoken, it is not impossible for you to understand each other. If you love each other and want your relationship to be successful, explore ways to balance your differences. Neither of you should feel uneasy.

Tiger and Dog

Your relationship has every possibility of success considering how capable the Dog is of going along with just about anything the Tiger wants to do. Conversely, the Tiger will probably find the Dog's antics a never-ending source of amusement and agree to most of the adventures the Dog proposes. Considering how imaginative and sexy you both are, there is no telling how much fun you can have together. However, if the Tiger somehow compromises or abuses the Dog, the Dog's bitter and pessimistic side will emerge and put the relationship in jeopardy. As long as the Tiger sees what a great friend the Dog can be, and treats the Dog with consideration and respect, everything will be fine. Because the two of you are intelligent and freedom-loving, your relationship can become highly creative. It can bring the best qualities out of both of you.

Tiger and Pig

While you have some basic differences, your relationship can be most interesting and intellectually productive, especially if the Pig is self-confident and supportive of the Tiger's aims. If the Tiger is willing to take this relationship seriously and be faithful, it will have, in addition to a rich source of natural wisdom, a sexy partner in the Pig. Nonetheless, if the Tiger takes the Pig for granted and fools around with others, the Pig will become deeply offended, and that could lead to some outrageous confrontations. While the Tiger can have a ferocious temper, it should never underestimate the Pig. Because the two of you can do great harm to each other, you need to make real efforts to understand yourselves and communicate. The two of you are capable of going to emotional extremes. The Pig is a caring and sensual creature who seeks to bond profoundly with its loved one. The Tiger, by contrast, is independent and autocratic. If you are willing to make allowances for each other's character traits, your relationship can be interesting and pleasurable for you both.

Rabbit and Rabbit

Because you have the same sign, you share many characteristics. The success of your relationship depends on how practical you are and how honestly you communicate with each other. The Rabbit is a complicated creature who is hard to know. It can appear to be perfectly calm while concealing its feelings. It is extremely sensitive and subtle, and is easily alarmed. Because it dreads intrusions, sudden changes, and confrontations, a relationship between two Rabbits can easily turn into a politely static affair. Nonetheless, the Rabbit is a very lovable and sexy creature. Because it adores all that is romantic, it can go out of its way to bestow affection on its beloved in a most endearing manner.

Rabbit and Dragon

This is a discordant combination. On the one hand, the abrupt and dynamic spirit of the Dragon alarms the elegant, comfort-loving Rabbit. On the other hand, the subtle and diplomatic Rabbit, who is an expert at politely sidestepping what it does not want to deal with, who dreads being disturbed, and who is so difficult to fathom, can exasperate the up-front Dragon. If the Rabbit's needs for privacy and tranquillity are challenged a bit too much and it becomes apprehensive, it might wander off to look for another relationship when the Dragon least expects it. Conversely, if the Dragon finds the Rabbit's elusive ways too frustrating and comes to the end of its tether, it might change its mind about the whole affair and kick the poor Rabbit out. Of course, if you make efforts to become objectively aware of each other's character traits and to accept and trust each other, you just might develop an enjoyable and interesting relationship.

Rabbit and Snake

Your chances for a pleasurable and peaceful relationship are excellent, especially if the Snake is emotionally supportive of the Rabbit. You have a great deal in common. You both are quiet, sensual, and luxury-loving. You are also content with simple things and can easily cooperate in creating the warm and secure home you both need. On the one hand, the Rabbit will find a wise and protective mate here, for the Snake is watchful and able to control the Rabbit's tendency to be insecure. On the other hand, the Snake can look forward to endless delights, for the Rabbit is one of the sexiest characters in the Chinese zodiac. The only danger in this combination is that you could sink into a state of convivial indolence unless life brings you a few interesting challenges.

Rabbit and Horse

If anyone can sweep the Rabbit off its feet, it surely is the Horse. Your relationship promises to be most interesting. Whether it lasts or not, however, is anyone's guess. Nothing, of course, is impossible, but the Horse, having found a wonderful playmate in the Rabbit, might be very surprised if the Rabbit ultimately trots off with someone else. The difficulty here is that, unless the Horse is able to give the Rabbit the security it requires, the Rabbit cannot be counted on to remain faithful. Not that the Horse can be counted on either; no character in the Chinese zodiac loves to roam more. While the Horse can love many people at once, the Rabbit can love only one at a time. When the Horse leaves it comes back, but when the Rabbit leaves it doesn't. If you want your relationship to hold together, you will have to develop a great deal of mutual understanding.

Rabbit and Sheep

This is an excellent combination. Your relationship will be most rewarding if the Rabbit befriends and stands by the Sheep. The Sheep, however, may find the Rabbit something of a riddle. Who takes better care of whom here is definitely an open question. You both are warm and kindhearted and inclined to put yourselves out for those you love. The riddle the Rabbit has for the Sheep is that it is a mysterious and elusive creature on the one hand and a sensual creature on the other. The best way the Sheep can accept the Rabbit is to let it be and enjoy all the loving attention it has to offer. Because the peace-loving Sheep is such a loyal creature, the Rabbit in all probability will not run away.

Rabbit and Monkey

Considering your pronounced differences, it is rather difficult to imagine how the two of you can get along. On the one hand, this combination challenges the Rabbit, who dreads confrontations, to take a positive stand and set definite boundaries, unless, of course, it really wants to be monkeyed with. On the other hand, this combination challenges the naturally curious and headstrong Monkey to give due consideration to the Rabbit's need for peace and quiet. Not that it's all bad; both of you are charmers and are very sexy. Nonetheless, the Monkey's need for constant excitement and inclination to dominate can make the Rabbit extremely insecure, while the Rabbit's need for absolute fidelity and tendency to smother its loved one can inspire the clever Monkey to find its way out of the Rabbit's warren. If you want your relationship to last, you will have to become aware of each other and make allowances for your different character traits.

Rabbit and Rooster

This is a difficult combination. If the Rabbit is looking for peace and quiet, it certainly is not going to find it with someone as persnickety and flamboyant as the Rooster. While you have a lot in common, your differences can drive you apart. Both of you are softhearted, affectionate, and sexy, and want to live in a secure and comfortable environment. However, the Rooster is always busy about something, and if its fussiness over details doesn't bring out the worst in the crafty Rabbit, its tendency to carp and enjoy a good squabble will. The Rabbit's need for peace and quiet, which at times makes it appear indifferent, can insult the chatty Rooster, who just hates to be ignored. If you want your relationship to work, you will have to become aware of yourselves and respect your natural differences.

Rabbit and Dog

Your relationship has possibilities for both good and bad. If the Rabbit values this relationship, it will have to take the courage to set its boundaries unless it wants to be provoked, and if the Dog values this relationship, it will have to respect the Rabbit's fondness for privacy. While you both are warmhearted and sexy, you are worriers and are not very good at decision making. The Dog's tendency to look for the trouble with everything and to be overanxious can make the Rabbit feel insecure. The Rabbit's tendency to hide what it thinks can make the Dog either suspicious or too curious for its own good. Still, if you want this relationship to work, look at the bright side: you both can be very playful and, if you love each other, can make a warm and secure home together.

Rabbit and Pig

This is an excellent combination. Because the Pig is so trustworthy and easy to get along with, the Rabbit can rest assured that it has a wonderful friend. Likewise, the Rabbit's genuine concern for the well-being and comfort of its loved one will make the Pig feel blessed. Both the Rabbit and the Pig are empathic. Because you intuitively understand how each other feels, your relationship will become more subtle and profound as time goes on. While you both thrive in peaceful surroundings, your sensual natures will make your relationship exciting and pleasurable, and because you place great value on loyalty, your relationship will most probably last a long time.

Dragon and Dragon

This is a difficult combination. Unless the two of you have an understanding, your relationship can easily become a spectacular battleground. One of you eventually will have to submit to the other. But how can a Dragon, who is naturally commanding, do that? Your relationship, therefore, is bound to be full of intrigue if not open conflict. The Dragon is very intelligent. It can easily conceal its aims and make the most surprising and deliberate moves. It hates restraints, will not back down, and is more than a match for its opponents. While the Dragon is always sincere in love, it is extremely demanding and easily frustrated. A revolutionary, the Dragon is always attracted to challenges. Perhaps that is why you have been drawn into this remarkable relationship to begin with.

Dragon and Snake

While an element of intrigue is inevitable in your relationship, it could work very nicely, especially if the Snake is willing to support the aims of the Dragon. Of course, it might take a bit of doing for the Snake to divine the Dragon's aims, considering how the Dragon always keeps its own counsel. But the Snake has its subtle ways and usually finds what it looks for. As long as the Dragon is true to the Snake, and gives it all the pleasure it wants, the Snake will be very happy. But if the Snake is wronged or betrayed, the Dragon will be in for quite a surprise. Be that as it may, both of you are usually sincere in love, if not possessive and jealous, and, while it is not beyond you to have some power struggles, you both have more than enough intelligence to make your relationship a success.

Dragon and Horse

This should prove to be a most interesting relationship. Considering how irrepressible you both are, you will get along either famously or not at all. The Horse is exuberant and restless. It is a changeable character, always on the go, and prone to emotional ups and downs. Because it is interested in all that is current, the Horse is usually well-informed and insightful, and, with its sense of humor and wonderful imagination, is able to hold its own in any exchange with the brilliant and intuitive Dragon. While the Horse is somewhat more imaginative than the Dragon, you are both excitable and passionate. As long as the Dragon is openhanded with the Horse, there should be no major trouble. But if the Horse gives the Dragon reason to become jealous, or if the Dragon tries to dominate the Horse, your relationship can come to a grinding halt. Obviously, the keys to the success of your relationship are trust and consideration for each other's needs. If you truly care for each other, there is no reason for your relationship not to last and be happy.

Dragon and Sheep

Considering the nature of your differences, you will get along very well as long as the Dragon is careful not to abuse the goodwill of the guileless Sheep. Because the Sheep is predisposed to want to be protected, the noble Dragon cannot help but hold an overpowering fascination for it. And because the Dragon is comfortable with quieter types, it will find an ideal companion in the Sheep. The Sheep is a deeply romantic and faithful soul who delights in being loved. The Dragon, however, is a dynamic character who will fight for what it wants in life and, although it means well, can go too far with its demands. Because the Dragon can unwittingly do a lot of damage to the relationship by walking all over the Sheep, the Sheep would be wise to overcome its timidity and define its limits, or boundaries, early.

Dragon and Monkey

This is an excellent combination. Nonetheless, because you both can be egotistical and aggressive, you will have to avoid certain pitfalls if you want your relationship to last. Because both of you can be imperious, it will be necessary for you to sort out your power issues. Ideally, you can rule the world together. However, when you are in strong disagreement you can have intense and drawn-out fights with serious repercussions unless you learn to steer a middle course. The least that can be said for your relationship is that you are bound to learn a great deal from each other. And if you learn to weather your storms well, it is certain that your love will always win the day.

Dragon and Rooster

While your personalities are quite different, the two of you can be very flamboyant. If the Dragon has a sense of humor, it may see how the fussy yet stylish Rooster is an ideal partner for it. As long as the Rooster is made to feel special, it will be happy and will go out of its way to make a lovely nest for its Dragon to live in. The Dragon's dramatic ways, sense of mastery, and influential manner cannot help but impress the critical Rooster, who loves to be in the presence of those it deems important. Likewise, the Rooster's cheerfulness, candor, and faithfulness will surely please the Dragon, who is both possessive and protective in love.

Dragon and Dog

This is a difficult combination. Because your natures are diametrically opposed, it is not likely that you will get along well unless you become aware of yourselves while making allowances for each other's different character traits. On the one hand, the Dog is a playful character. It hates to make up its mind and tends to become cynical, especially if hurt. On the other hand, the Dragon is not as playful as it is shrewd. It is often visionary. It knows precisely what it wants and will fight to have its way, no matter what the cost. The Dog, out of its natural sportive-ness, will go along with the Dragon, but only up to a point. When the Dog shows the Dragon that it has a mind of its own, it is most unlikely that the intrepid Dragon will go along with the Dog. You will save your relationship a lot of trouble if the Dog firmly maintains its boundaries from the start, and if the Dragon recognizes that its views are not the only ones in the universe.

Dragon and Pig

While one might question how the voracious Dragon and the succulent Pig could ever get along in a way that is not to the Pig's disadvantage, it is possible if you make efforts to understand and accept your different character traits. Considering how vulnerable the Pig is, it must overcome its inability to say no and learn to set sane boundaries if it doesn't want to be hurt by the unwitting and robust Dragon. For its part, the Dragon should treat the Pig in a protective and nonabusive way unless it wants to drive the Pig to despair and force it to defend itself, which it can do quite savagely. If you love each other you can do a great deal of good for each other. The Pig is a deeply sensual and caring soul who can provide the Dragon with a warm and loving environment. The Dragon is a passionate, courageous, and sincere character who can easily provide the Pig with the secure and loving conditions it needs to feel happy.

Snake and Snake

Because you have the same sign, you share many of the same positive and negative characteristics. The success of your relationship depends not only on how well you know yourselves but on whether you keep your agreements. The snake is a sensual and luxury-loving creature, fond of sex and ease. While you are sociable and gracious, you tend to be secretive and always keep your own counsel. Because you are possessive and jealous in love, and inclined to hold sway over your mate, the two of you probably will have to sort out your power issues carefully if you want to avoid trouble down the road. Under stress the Snake can be quick to take offense. If one of you betrays or crosses the other, the other may become vengeful. Notwithstanding, if you form loving bonds and are comfortable with each other, it is unlikely that you will ever grow apart.

Snake and Horse

How far you two go together depends on what sorts of demands you make on each other. While you may find each other fascinating and sexually attractive, you are very dissimilar. The Snake no doubt is fascinated by the Horse's exuberance and imagination. But the Snake requires stability; it needs its mate to be constant if it is going to be happy. The Snake is a sensual and pleasure-loving creature who is perfectly content to live a quiet, stable, even sedentary way of life. The Horse, by contrast, thrives on change. It needs constant movement and variety and cannot bear to be restrained. Because the Horse is a mercurial soul who has countless interests and is easily tempted, it cannot help but arouse the Snake's jealousy. Of course, if the Snake is up for adventure, this relationship might work. There's always the chance, especially if the Snake controls its tendency to be possessive and knows just how to butter up the Horse, that the Horse will look forward to coming home to the stable at the end of the day.

Snake and Sheep

If the guileless Sheep confides in the Snake and seeks its advice, the wise old Snake will be very happy indeed. On the one hand, the Snake, who loves to manage the affairs of those it loves, will find a wonderful partner in the loyal and tenderhearted Sheep. On the other hand, the affectionate Sheep will find a marvelous companion in the Snake, who is not only intelligent and caring but extremely sensual and graceful. While problems can develop between you, especially if the Snake is one of the more possessive and domineering types and the Sheep is one of the more independent types, it is unlikely that you will ever go apart if you truly love each other. Your life together may become so peaceful and quiet that your communication will be telepathic.

Snake and Monkey

This is a difficult combination. Depending on how you understand each other, your relationship will become either a battle of wits or a lot of fun. While both of you are intelligent and pleasure-loving, you will have to deal with certain problems inherent in the combination of your signs if you want your relationship to last. Because you both tend to be domineering and clever, you can resort to every trick in the book to get your ways. The Monkey is a restless character who loves excitement and lots of talk. The Snake, by contrast, doesn't let on half of what it thinks. While communication problems can easily develop between you, the Snake's reticence will surely intensify the Monkey's curiosity, which the Snake can use to lead the Monkey by the nose if it wants to. Because the Monkey's restlessness will raise the Snake's suspicions, the Snake will also tend to spy on the Monkey's moves. If the Monkey betrays or otherwise offends the Snake, the Snake might become enraged. While the possibility of havoc is real in your relationship, the possibility of peace is also. If you respect and care for each other and are sincere in your agreements, there is no reason why the two of you cannot be very happy together.

Snake and Rooster

This is an excellent combination. Because the qualities of your signs blend in a way that makes your relationship richly productive, it is almost certain that you will be able to go through life together in peace and prosperity. While the Snake will inevitably rule the roost, the Rooster will be perfectly content to keep the Snake as snug as a bug. Because the discerning Snake knows what a treasure its Rooster is, it will also know just what to say to make the softhearted Rooster feel well-loved and cared for. Because there certainly will be the occasional squabble, which the Rooster will enjoy, as it will inevitably arouse the Snake's sexual passion, the two of you will always get along famously. You both are extremely pleasure-loving and endowed with big sexual appetites.

Snake and Dog

Considering how adaptable you both are, there is no reason why you can't stay together a long time. The chances for the success of your relationship will be all the greater if the Snake is emotionally supportive of the Dog. Considering the innate wisdom of the Snake, this should not be a problem. In all probability the Snake will have the upper hand in this match, so the Dog's tendency to be irresolute will give way to the Snake's intentions. Because of this, the activity of your relationship should settle down to a steady rhythm, in which the enjoyment of sensual pleasures plays a major part. The only danger here is that the Dog may become bored unless the Snake can interrupt its routines and go away for an occasional adventure together.

Snake and Pig

This is a difficult combination. While both of you are quiet and sensual, you have subtle and profound differences that can undermine your relationship unless you become aware of them. It is essential for Snake to be sure of its intentions and be perfectly candid with the Pig. The Pig would do well to restrain its generous impulse and need to bond in love in order to give this relationship time to develop. While both of you place great importance on loyalty, the Snake can move much more shrewdly than the Pig. If the Snake is discontented with its financial circumstances and doubts that the Pig can offer it the security or status it wants for the future, it can maneuver behind the Pig's back in ways that will put the Pig at a serious disadvantage. If the Pig is hurt badly enough, however, it will react savagely and harm the Snake. It is necessary, therefore, for you both to communicate candidly and responsibly from the outset of your relationship in order to avoid serious misunderstandings. The watchword for your combination is caution.

Horse and Horse

This is a difficult combination. While you certainly can share wonderful times, considering how playful and imaginative you are, it might be difficult for you to stay on course together. The Horse is a sociable and spontaneous character. It has a lot of friendly acquaintances, but, like the proverbial rolling stone, it keeps few lasting relationships. Two Horses will talk up a storm and have lots of laughs. But, because neither will follow the other for very long, they will tend to drift apart unless they have real reasons to stay together and agree on their individual needs for autonomy. Another potential problem is that, because the Horse tends to want the admiration and support of its social circle to feel special, two Horses can compete for attention, especially if they are mates. This relationship, in spite of its pitfalls, can work if you generate tolerance for each other and choose to be faithful through all the changes life brings your way.

Horse and Sheep

While the two of you have noticeably different personalities, you can get along well and be the best of friends. Because the open and talkative Horse can easily get the taciturn Sheep to open up and tell what's on its mind, you are capable of achieving a depth of understanding that few people ever know. The imaginative Sheep can fascinate the Horse with the depth of its thoughts, while the Horse can delight the Sheep with its surprising insights. While the Sheep has a much greater love of home than the Horse, the two of you share a love of adventure and can be happy traveling to exotic and wild places together. If you consider living together, you would do yourselves a great favor if you found a large place. It also is necessary, if you want your relationship to last, for the Sheep to let the Horse come and go as it will, and for the Horse to be completely trustworthy and loyal to the Sheep.

Horse and Monkey

If the Monkey thinks it can break in the Horse, it had better think twice. Because the Horse is just as much a leader as the Monkey, it will do only what it wants to do. The Horse is a wild and spirited creature who often acts impulsively. Should the headstrong Monkey succeed in dominating the Horse, however, it will come to have regrets. The Monkey should ask itself if the exuberant passion of the Horse attracts it or if the prospect of conquest challenges it. While the Monkey is a shrewd and practical character, it can learn a great deal if, instead of trying to force its will upon the Horse, it opens itself to the Horse's imaginative point of view. If you learn to accept and live with each other's different character traits, you will have a wonderful relationship. You are both fun-loving and humorous, and would make great traveling companions through life's adventures.

Horse and Rooster

While there is no essential discord between your signs, it is hard to see how the two of you can easily get along, considering the Horse's jovial if slapdash manner and the Rooster's meticulousness. The Horse is an exuberant and restless character who loves variety, has a million interests, and is almost always on the go. The

Rooster, while it certainly loves novelty, is a critical and selective character with strong nesting instincts. Because the Rooster is generally careful in making choices, it takes a long time to decide to give itself in a relationship. Loyalty is extremely important for the Rooster. Loyalty is also important for the Horse, but the Horse does not see it at all the same way. The last thing the Horse wants is to be cooped up. If the Horse and Rooster are to get along, the Rooster will have to give the Horse the space it really needs. Conversely, the Horse will have to internalize some of its desire to roam so that it doesn't leave the Rooster feeling neglected and lonely.

Horse and Dog

This is an excellent combination. Considering how warmhearted and imaginative you both are, and how well you can travel together, your relationship, despite problems that might come up along the way, has every chance of working. While the Horse's emotional ups and downs can worry the Dog, the Dog is adaptable and responds positively to the Horse's restlessness and need to be on the go. Never can it be said that the Dog is unwilling to go along for a good ride. Life between the Dog and the Horse is often high-spirited and filled with happiness. Because you make such a winning couple, you have the luck of attracting people who are willing and able to open doors for you and help you achieve your highest aims in life.

Horse and Pig

While there is no essential discord between your signs, it is hard to imagine how the two of you can get along easily, considering how different your needs are. Neither of you has a mean bone in your body, but it will be difficult for you to avoid coming to some frustrating misunderstandings. The Horse is a restless character who loves to travel and won't be held down. While the Horse is very loving, it needs frequent change and excitement. It can't be counted on to be constant, at least in the sense the Pig understands. The Pig is a nurturing and empathic character who, because it has the worst time saying no, is prone to getting hurt. In love the Pig refuses nothing and wants nothing more than to form deep and lasting bonds. Because both of you are apt to experience emotional extremes, you will be heading for a great deal of conflict unless you proceed carefully and make due allowances for each other's needs.

Sheep and Sheep

Because you have the same sign, you have many of the same positive and negative characteristics. One might assume that it is easy for the two of you to get along, but because the Sheep tends to become nervous you can develop some distressing problems in your relationship unless you are perfectly candid about your mutual intentions. This may not be so easy, however. The Sheep is a shy creature who often conceals its deeper thoughts. It takes a great deal of time and developing of trust for a Sheep to open up fully, even though it loves to be close. The Sheep is naturally romantic. You can care very deeply and tenderly for each other. Because you are attracted to peaceful and quiet environments, you can create a beautiful and serene home, and enjoy traveling to romantic places together.

Sheep and Monkey

While it is possible for you to have a lot of fun together, it is also possible for you to arrive at an impasse if your relationship becomes a one-way street. The Sheep is a warmhearted soul who can't help but love the fascinating Monkey. Likewise, the Monkey, who has a soft spot in its heart for those who praise it, can't help but adore the admiring Sheep. The Monkey is a gregarious character whose independent ways can unsettle the more or less stay-at-home Sheep. However, because the Sheep is faithful to the one it loves, the Monkey will always treat it with a great deal of affection. Trouble can develop, however, if the regal Monkey starts forcing its will on the Sheep. The Sheep, while it is a tolerant and peace-loving soul, has its limit. If it is abused or shown too much disrespect, it will react. If the Sheep fights in earnest with the Monkey, it will be extremely difficult to revive the relationship. It takes a great deal to gain the genuine confidence of the Sheep.

Sheep and Rooster

Considering how harmoniously your signs combine with each other, your relationship should be truly peaceful and loving, unless, of course, the Rooster's fussiness gets on the Sheep's nerves, or the Sheep's taciturnity offends the chatty Rooster. If the Sheep gives the Rooster emotional support, however, by showing it the sort of loving attention it needs, the Rooster in turn will make the Sheep feel blessed. There is no character more tenderhearted and loving in the Chinese zodiac than the Rooster. Both of you tend to be devoted to loved ones and give much importance to your home. The Rooster is the more practical one. It is capable of organizing the household down to the finest detail. The Sheep is a dreamer. It can create a most romantic atmosphere. If you arrange your home together, therefore, it will be a beautiful and peaceful place.

Sheep and Dog

This is a difficult combination. While your signs don't appear on the surface to disagree, there are areas where you could run into some trouble. You both tend to be worriers. In your concern to make each other happy, you could inadvertently stir up an undercurrent of anxiety that could take much of the joy out of your relationship. Because it can take the coy Sheep a long time to say what it wants or doesn't want, the Sheep can't be of much help to the Dog when it comes time to make decisions. Anyway, the Dog tends not to like to have to make decisions. It anxiously looks for everything that could go wrong. If the Dog is the sort who is given to chattering nervously about everything that troubles it, it can drive the equally nervous but far more reticent Sheep to distraction. Nonetheless, the two of you can avoid your pitfalls. Just be patient with life and look at the brighter side of your relationship: you both are loyal and honest, and capable of showing each other great tenderness.

Sheep and Pig

This excellent pairing of signs clearly indicates that your relationship, in spite of any problems that might arise, has every chance of success. Because both of you are naturally empathic, you can understand each other's feelings without having to ask many questions. Considering how adaptable you are, it is easy for you to bring all the areas of your lives together in harmony. It is also no problem for either of you to be flexible and make special efforts to accommodate each other. Your home, while it might not be the neatest place in the world, will surely be the happiest and most comfortable. Considering how romantically inclined and imaginative you both are, you would do well to live in beautiful surroundings. You would be most peaceful if you lived in the country or by the sea.

Monkey and Monkey

Because you have the same sign, you share many positive and negative characteristics. To say the least, your relationship will always be filled with excitement. You can have outrageously good times as well as outrageous arguments. The Monkey is a magnetic character. It is generally fun-loving, talkative, affectionate, and sexy, and absolutely loves to have others sing its praises. It also is a regal type. Because it can be headstrong, cunning, and aggressive, and will force its way if necessary, it invites opposition. Expecting a Monkey to give in without a good fight is really asking too much. If you want your relationship to be civil, cultivate your talents for diplomacy, and by all means don't take yourselves too seriously.

Monkey and Rooster

While there is nothing essentially discordant about the combination of your signs, you do have differences that deserve your attention. You both are alert and resourceful, and have the strength to achieve whatever goals you envision. However, the well-organized Rooster can irritate the Monkey by its obsessive attention to details, and the restless Monkey can fluster the Rooster by its talent for engineering sweeping changes and making bold and sudden moves. The Rooster, who needs consistency, can become harshly critical of the Monkey. The Monkey can become extremely impatient and insult the Rooster. You both tend to be outspoken and egotistical. Nonetheless, if you work on balancing and integrating your differences, you will be able to enjoy what you do have in common. Both of you are warmhearted. You love to attract attention and need to be praised. Therefore, if you show loving attention to each other, and praise each other for all the good and beautiful qualities you certainly have, you will make each other very happy indeed.

Monkey and Dog

Because of the way your signs work together, you have excellent chances of a loving relationship filled with interesting adventures and developments. There is no end to what you can share. You both are fun-loving, sociable, curious, and talkative. While the Dog is apt to accommodate the rather willful Monkey, the Monkey, as it gets to know the Dog, will be more and more inclined to rely on the Dog's remarkable intuition and sense of judgment. Because you balance each other very well, there is an easy give-and-take dynamic to your relationship. Considering how big your sexual appetites are, and how readily you reward each other's loyalty with affection, it is only natural for you to have a happy and productive life together.

Monkey and Pig

While your signs can integrate very well with each other, they do have some differences that can be rather bewildering at times. If you want your relationship to go smoothly, the Monkey will have to be honest and considerate of the Pig's feelings, and the Pig will have to know when to say no. If the Pig is looking for the kind of relationship in which it can bond or merge with its mate and not have to look out for itself, it certainly is in for a surprise. If the Monkey is looking for a lot of excitement, notwithstanding the Pig's amazing sex appeal, it may be in for a surprise as well, especially if it doesn't play by the rules. Your essential difference is in your temperaments. The Monkey lives in its intuition and intellect. The Pig, while also very intelligent, lives more in its feelings and emotions. Because the Monkey has the power to support the Pig's emotions, it is important for it to listen to what the Pig needs to be happy, which is actually quite simple. Likewise, because the Pig has the power to support the Monkey's inspirations, it is important for it to listen to what the Monkey has on its mind. If you find the way to balance each other's proclivities, your relationship will become rich and pleasurable.

Rooster and Rooster

This is a difficult combination. One might think that two Roosters, having so much in common, would get along perfectly well, but considering what a perfectionist the Rooster is, it might not be all that easy. Unless you are in perfect agreement, or are able to develop expert negotiating skills, you could easily offend each other from time to time. Even so, considering your penchant for obsessing over details, you could use whatever negotiating skills you develop to torture each other. Not that the Rooster is a perverse or ill-humored creature; the Rooster is actually softhearted, if not a little vain. It is really because the Rooster is so fastidious and critical that problems can grow like crabgrass when the two of you are living under the same roof. Of course, if you manage to establish a workable pecking order, your relationship might turn out to be a joy. The Rooster is an affectionate and loyal creature who has a big sexual appetite. You both need to be praised. Therefore, it will help your relationship a lot if you look at the bright side. Praise each other for all your beauty and wit, and enjoy the warmth and comfort you can give each other.

Rooster and Dog

While this is an essentially discordant combination, it is possible for you to get along perfectly well. Much depends on what kind of interest the Dog takes in the Rooster's emotional needs. At first glance this does not appear to be difficult for the Dog, considering how affectionate and easygoing it can be. But that's exactly where the trouble lies. The meticulous Rooster can become annoyed by the Dog's ways. While the Dog is often content to handle whatever it considers unimportant with a lick and a promise, the Rooster is extremely detail-oriented. When the Rooster's sense of order is disturbed, it becomes upset, even harshly critical. If the Rooster were to play down its tendency to fret, which, by the way, can torment the Dog, it would give the relationship every chance of succeeding. You both are softhearted and sexy, and place great value on fidelity.

Rooster and Pig

While there is no essential discord between your signs, your relationship could develop a number of unnecessary problems unless the Rooster finds a way to take the jovial Pig under its wing and the Pig manages to countenance the often critical Rooster. Considering how kindhearted and sensual you both are, this should not be too difficult. If given free rein, however, the Pig will go to a depth of emotionality that the Rooster probably will not be able to fathom, while the Rooster will aim for a level of intellectual precision that the Pig will find too limiting. The

Rooster is also very talkative, while the Pig is often silent. Communication, therefore, will not be easy unless you both make allowances for your differences without taking them personally.

Dog and Dog

Because you have the same sign you share many of the same positive and negative characteristics. Essentially, you should get along very easily. However, if you give in to your tendencies to be indecisive and anxious about the future, you could lose you way. The Dog's nature is not simple. It can be playful and affectionate on the one hand and pessimistic on the other. Because the Dog is prone to anxiety, it has trouble making up its mind, even though it has excellent judgment and is capable of working hard to attain whatever it wants. The Dog is loyal and honest, especially when in love. Therefore, if you truly love each other, there is no reason why you can't have everything you want together as long as you decide to go forward come what may.

Dog and Pig

Owing to the essential nature of your two signs, you can share a deep level of experience. While your temperaments are somewhat different, you both are capable of experiencing a wide range of feelings. Because you both are playful, you can have some riotously good times together. However, you can become very somber and moody. Depending on how well you understand yourselves, your relationship can be deeply satisfying or head for dangerous waters. The Dog's anxious and pessimistic side can really trouble the Pig, while the Pig's profound silences can unnerve the Dog. Nonetheless, the Pig can always be counted on to relate exactly what it feels, and the Dog can appeal easily to the Pig's imagination. The best way to ensure the happiness of this relationship is for the Dog to play down its tendency to worry and for the Pig to feel encouraged. Because you both are pleasure-loving, your best communication is when you are in each other's arms.

Pig and Pig

While yours is a difficult combination, there is no reason why you can't have a

deeply meaningful relationship, unless, of course, you are harboring a lot of unresolved pain from your pasts. You both are complex and moody. Nonetheless, you are purehearted and jovial, and will deny nothing to each other if you truly love each other. You can love totally and openly, and, because you find it so hard to say no, you are vulnerable to abuse. While it is most unlikely that either of you is willing to abuse the other, you can vent a great deal of rage at each other if you have not resolved the frustrations of your past relationships. Besides the fact that your sign is the most sensual of them all, it indicates that you are capable of deep reflection. If you are patient, and give each other the space to reflect quietly, especially when in a dark mood, your relationship will thrive.

Your Element Compatibility

Let's look now at how the elements that qualify your animal signs relate. You will remember that you were born not just in the time of the Rat, Ox, Tiger, and so on but in the time of the Wood Rat, Fire Rat, Earth Rat, and so forth. Because a Wood Rat gets along somewhat differently with a Fire Snake than with an Earth Snake, we need to look more closely at your compatibilities. In reading through the following element compatibilities, remember: if your animal sign is in harmony with the animal sign of your partner, the elements that head your respective animal signs will either enhance or compromise that harmony. Conversely, if your animal signs are out of harmony, their respective elements will either intensify or ease that disharmony.

Wood and Wood

If the element of both your and your partner's year or day of birth is Wood, you will be in perfect accord, providing that one of you has yin Wood and the other has yang Wood. If both of you have either yin or yang Wood, you will tend to clash from time to time.

Wood and Fire

If the element of your year or day of birth is Wood and the element of your partner's year or day of birth is Fire, you will be in harmony, and you will tend to be supportive of your partner, as Wood supports Fire.

Wood and Earth

If the element of your year or day of birth is Wood and the element of your partner's year or day of birth is Earth, your relationship will have an element of discord. However, if the element of your day of birth is Wood and the element of your partner's day of birth is Earth, while your style of relating, as determined in Chapter 2, is yang and your partner's style of relating is yin, you will get along perfectly well.

Wood and Metal

If the element of your year or day of birth is Wood and the element of your partner's year or day of birth is Metal, your relationship will have an element of discord. However, if the element of your day of birth is Wood and the element of your partner's day of birth is Metal, while your style of relating, as determined in Chapter 2, is yin and your partner's style of relating is yang, you will get along perfectly well.

Wood and Water

If the element of your year or day of birth is Wood and the element of your partner's year or day of birth is Water, you will be in harmony, and your partner will tend to be supportive of you, as Water supports Wood.

Fire and Fire

If the element of both your and your partner's year or day of birth is Fire, you will be in perfect accord, providing that one of you has yin Fire and the other has yang Fire. If both of you have either yin or yang Fire, you will tend to clash from time to time.

Fire and Earth

If the element of your year or day of birth is Fire and the element of your partner's year or day of birth is Earth, you will be in harmony, and you will tend to be supportive of your partner, as Fire supports Earth.

Fire and Metal

If the element of your year or day of birth is Fire and the element of your partner's year or day of birth is Metal, your relationship will have an element of discord. However, if the element of your day of birth is Fire and the element of your partner's day of birth is Metal, while your style of relating, as determined in Chapter 2, is yang and your partner's is yin, you will get along perfectly well.

Fire and Water

If the element of your year or day of birth is Fire and the element of your partner's year or day of birth is Metal, your relationship will have an element of discord. However, if the element of your day of birth is Fire and the element of your partner's day of birth is Water, while your style of relating, as determined in Chapter 2, is yin and your partner's is yang, you will get along perfectly well.

Earth and Earth

If the element of both your and your partner's year or day of birth is Earth, you will be in perfect accord, providing that one of you has yin Earth and the other has yang Earth. If both of you have either yin or yang Earth, you will tend to clash from time to time.

Earth and Metal

If the element of your year or day of birth is Earth and the element of your partner's year or day of birth is Metal, you will be in harmony, and you will tend to be supportive of your partner, as Earth supports Metal.

Earth and Water

If the element of your year or day of birth is Earth and the element of your partner's year or day of birth is Water, your relationship will have an element of discord. However, if the element of your day of birth is Earth and the element of your partner's day of birth is Water, while your style of relating, as determined in Chapter 2, is yang and your partner's is yin, you will get along perfectly well.

Metal and Metal

If the element of both your and your partner's year or day of birth is Metal, you will be in perfect accord, providing that one of you has yin Metal and the other has yang Metal. If both of you have either yin or yang Metal, you will tend to clash from time to time.

Metal and Water

If the element of your year or day of birth is Metal and the element of your partner's year or day of birth is Water, you will be in harmony, and you will tend to be supportive of your partner, as Metal supports Water.

Water and Water

If the element of both your and your partner's year and day of birth is Water, you will be in perfect accord, providing that one of you has yin Water and the other has yang Water. If both of you have either yin or yang Water, you will tend to clash from time to time.

Exercise

First compare the element and animal sign of your year of birth with those of your partner. Then compare the element and animal sign of your day of birth with those of your partner, giving slightly stronger emphasis to the day. Try to synthesize the meanings of these combinations.

If you have discordant combinations, they don't mean that your relationship won't work, any more than harmonious combinations guarantee success. We all are in relationships to learn from each other. While the comparisons of your signs and elements may point out various positive or negative possibilities, it is unwise to attribute your problems to things outside yourself. Or, as Shakespeare so rightly put it, "The fault, dear Brutus, is not in our stars, but in ourselves."

In Part Two, you will learn how to use the material in your Personal Data list in arranging the feng shui of your home to attract the conditions that you want in your life. If you have left anything in your Personal Data list blank, please fill it in now, before going on to Part Two.

Creating a Loving Environment

How to Use Part Two

You are just about ready to begin applying your personal data to arranging the feng shui of your home. But first there are a few practical details that you will need to grasp to work with the material in the coming chapters. They are fully delineated here.

How to Draw Your Floor Plan

If you already have an architectural drawing of your home, you won't have to draw it yourself. If it is very large, however, bring it to a photocopy shop and have it reduced to a size that is easy to handle—8½ by 11 is fine. Make several copies for the sake of convenience.

If you don't have an architectural drawing of your home, you will have to draw it yourself. Your drawing doesn't have to be exact, but it should be reasonably correct. You can draw it most easily on graph paper. If you don't want to take the dimensions of your home with a tape measure, simply pace out its length and breadth, estimating about three feet to each step. Try to draw your floor plan on an 8½-x-11-inch sheet of paper and, again, you'll want to make several photocopies of it.

Please note that your home, or living space, is nothing more than your private space. If you live in an apartment building, your home is your apartment, not the building. If you rent a room in an apartment or a residence hotel, your home or private living quarters is your room, not the apartment or residence hotel. If you live in a house and are its owner, your home is the entire house. This is an important matter. When arranging the feng shui of your home, deal only with your space, as determined by the door that marks the boundary between you and the rest of the world.

Determining the Central Point of Your Home

The central point of your home is like a hub. Because it is so important for many of the procedures that we will be doing, you will need to mark it on your floor plan. If your floor plan is a simple rectangle or square, this will be very easy to do. Just pencil in diagonal lines from corner to corner, as illustrated in figure 1 below. The central point is where the two diagonal lines cross.

(fig. 1)

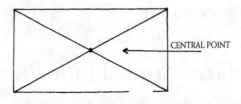

CENTRAL POINT

If your floor plan has an irregular pattern, extend its lines until they form a rectangle or square, as illustrated in figures 2 and 3. Then pencil in the diagonal lines to find the central point.

(fig. 2) 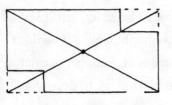   *(fig. 3)*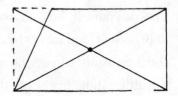

Reading the Compass

To read a compass correctly, stand facing squarely toward the direction you want to determine. Hold your compass level in front of you. Turn the whole compass case in your hand until the north end of the needle points to the letter *N* on the azimuth ring. (The azimuth ring is the ring of degrees—north, east, south, and west—printed on the plate of your compass.) The north end of the needle is either coated with green phosphorus or marked *N*. The earth's magnetic field causes the needle to point toward the magnetic North Pole. To find your bearing, just read the direction and degree straight ahead of you on the azimuth ring of the compass.

Determining the Element of Your Doorway

Your main doorway faces one of the eight compass directions (north, northeast, east, southeast, south, southwest, west, or northwest), which corresponds to one of the five elements. The element to which your door is aligned is the element that rules your home. To determine this element, you need to take a compass reading of your principal door. To do so, stand in your doorway facing squarely *out*. The direction on your compass indicates the door's element. If your home has more than one entrance, take a reading of the doorway you use most commonly.

- If your door faces **north**, your home is ruled by the element Water.
- If your door faces **northeast**, your home is ruled by the element Earth.
- If your door faces **east**, your home is ruled by the element Wood.
- If your door faces **southeast**, your home is ruled by the element Wood.
- If your door faces **south**, your home is ruled by the element Fire.
- If your door faces **southwest**, your home is ruled by the element Earth.
- If your door faces **west**, your home is ruled by the element Metal.
- If your door faces **northwest**, your home is ruled by the element Metal.

If the direction you are facing appears to be between two compass directions, refer to figure 4 to determine which is correct. You can see that north extends from 337.30 to 22.30; northeast from 22.30 to 67.30; east from 67.30 to 112.30; southeast from 112.30 to 157.30; south from 157.30 to 202.30; southwest from 202.30 to 247.30; west from 247.30 to 292.30; and northwest from 292.30 to 337.30.

(fig. 4)

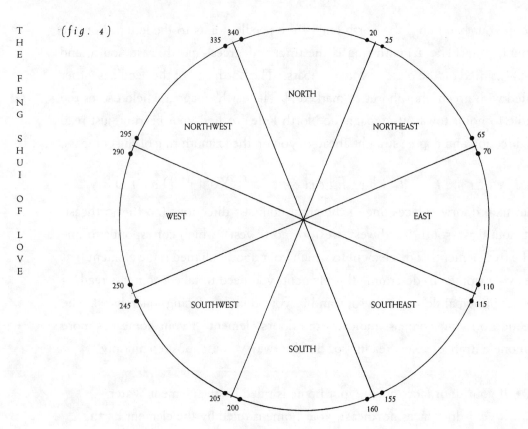

Demarcating the Directions of Your Floor Plan

The way to determine the compass directions in your floor plan always begins with noting the compass direction of the main door. This is because the compass direction of the main door is exactly the same as the direction you face when looking toward the front wall from the central point of the space. For example, if your doorway faced north, the direction you would be facing, while standing at the central point of your home and looking toward the front wall, would also be north, whether the doorway was directly in front of the central point or not. Figure 5 illustrates this.

Once you have determined the compass direction of the front wall from the perspective of the central point of your floor plan, you are ready to determine the rest of the eight compass directions. To do this properly, divide out the space by drawing eight spokes from the central point of your floor plan, as illustrated in figure 6.

132

(fig. 5)

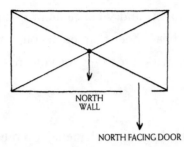

NORTH
WALL

NORTH FACING DOOR

Once you have demarcated the eight areas, write in their compass directions. Figure 7 shows all eight directions for a space whose doorway faces north. Whichever direction your door faces, refer to figure 7 to help you fill out the different compass directions around your space. Note that the sequence of directions always rotates clockwise: north, northeast, east, southeast, south, southwest, west, and northwest.

(fig. 6)   (fig. 7)

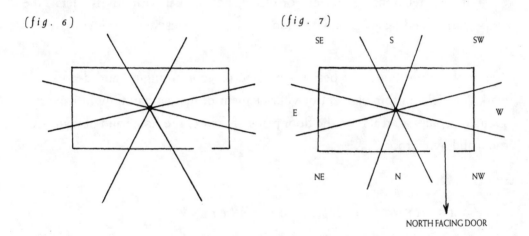

SE   S   SW

E   W

NE   N   NW

NORTH FACING DOOR

The Relationship Element and the Element of Mutual Harmony

When noting the compass directions of your relationship element and your element of mutual harmony, first work with the floor plan of your whole house, then use separate floor plans for individual rooms, especially the bedroom and the living room. For individual rooms, first make a floor plan. Next, determine its central point. Then find the compass direction of its door and mark off the compass areas as you did on the floor plan of your whole house.

Your relationship element and your element of mutual harmony, as determined in Chapter 4, should have been entered in your Personal Data list. Following are the corresponding compass directions for your relationship element and element of mutual harmony.

- If your relationship element or element of mutual harmony is Water, the corresponding area on your floor plan is the north.
- If your relationship element or element of mutual harmony is Wood, the corresponding areas on your floor plan are the east and southeast.
- If your relationship element or element of mutual harmony is Fire, the corresponding area on your floor plan is the south.
- If your relationship element or element of mutual harmony is Earth, the corresponding areas on your floor plan are the northeast and southwest.
- If your relationship element or element of mutual harmony is Metal, the corresponding areas on your floor plan are the west and northwest.

As these positions will bear upon some of your arranging and decorating, mark your relationship element or your element of mutual harmony in its corresponding compass area(s) on the floor plans of your entire home and of your bedroom and living room.

Your Area of Special Interest

The way to find the compass direction of your area of special interest is not different from the way you found the compass directions of your relationship element and element of mutual harmony. When noting the compass direction of your area of special interest, work with the floor plan of your entire home first, then work with the floor plan of an appropriate room according to your area of special interest. Use common sense in determining the appropriate room.

- If your area of special interest corresponds to the element Water, its appropriate direction in space is north.

- If your area of special interest corresponds to the element Wood, its appropriate directions in space are east and southeast.
- If your area of special interest corresponds to the element Fire, its appropriate direction in space is south.
- If your area of special interest corresponds to the element Earth, its appropriate directions in space are northeast and southwest.
- If your area of special interest corresponds to the element Metal, its appropriate directions in space are west and northwest.

Mark your area of special interest in its appropriate places on your floor plans.

Compass Alignment of Bed, Couch, and Chair

A bed is judged by the direction toward which its head is pointing. To find out, take your compass and stand at the foot of the bed, facing the head. The direction indicated by your compass is your bed's alignment. For example, if you are standing at the foot of your bed, squarely facing the head, and you get a compass reading of east, your bed's alignment is to the east.

Chairs and couches are judged by their backs. Take your compass and stand in front of and squarely facing a chair. The direction indicated by your compass is your chair's alignment. Figures 8 and 9 illustrate how to read the alignments of a bed and a chair. Notice the direction the arrows point, indicating how you are to stand.

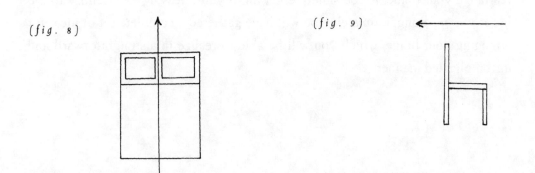

(fig. 8)

(fig. 9)

Locating the Marriage Point
on Your Floor Plan

The marriage point is not a compass point. It is always determined by standing in the doorway and looking *into* the space. The marriage point is always to the far right-hand corner of any space, as illustrated in figure 10.

(*fig. 10*)

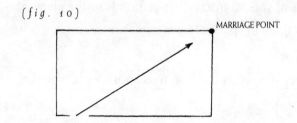

MARRIAGE POINT

On your floor plan, first mark down the marriage point of your entire home. Then mark down the marriage points of your bedroom and your living room.

As we progress through Part Two, you will see how all of this material comes into play. If anywhere along the way you find yourself in doubt about how to read the compass, how to determine the compass direction of a doorway, or the like, please refer back to the instructions in this section to refresh your memory.

As you read through the coming chapters, you will find many ideas and solutions for arranging your home that you will want to remember, so set aside a few blank sheets of paper on which you can list these solutions. I shall refer to this list as your Things to Do list.

Please read all of the material in Part Two before you actually begin to rearrange your home. If you simply enter all of your ideas in your Things to Do list as you go along, ultimately you will have gathered a complete set of ideas for arranging your home, which you will be able to realize in a straightforward and uncomplicated manner.

chapter 8

The Overall Arrangement of Your Home

Whether you live alone, as a couple, or as a family, there are a few broad concepts that you can utilize to give your home a well-balanced and comfortable feeling. When reading through these concepts, try to envision how you could use them. You might want to make some rough sketches and notes as you go along.

The Flow of Chi

Chi flows like wind and water. It flows along the contours of your home. It enters through the door and flows out and back through the windows. It also enters your home from the ground below and the sky above. Ideally, it should flow through your home smoothly and calmly, neither rushing nor becoming stagnant. Chi tends to rush through long, narrow corridors and stagnate in places obstructed by furniture that is too big and by clutter.

Chi is cyclic in nature. It oscillates. The valleys and peaks of its oscillations are yin and yang. When you look at your home in terms of yin and yang, you can see how the front is yang and the back is yin; the brighter areas are yang and the darker areas are yin; the more active areas are yang and the more restful areas are yin; the more public areas are yang and the more private areas are yin; the living room, dining room, kitchen, family room, den, and home office are yang, and the bedrooms and bathrooms are yin.

Yin and Yang Areas of the Home

Yin	Yang
Back	Front
Shade	Light
Restful	Active
Private	Public
Bedrooms, bathrooms	Living room, dining room, kitchen, family room, den, home office

When yin and yang are brought into harmonious balance, chi flows smoothly and without obstruction and life flourishes. Whether you live in a studio, a one-bedroom apartment, or a larger home, if you bring its yin and yang aspects into harmony, it will encourage and support positive developments in your life and relationships.

It is important, especially in a studio apartment, to differentiate private and shared areas. Because a studio is so open, these differences can be quite subtle. The most private area in a studio is farthest from the door yet away from the windows. You can create or enhance a feeling of privacy around your sleeping area by using a screen or piece of furniture such as a sofa or dresser, or by hanging a curtain near the bed. Be careful, however, not to crowd the area around the bed. If your studio apartment is small, an excellent solution for the sleeping area would be to install a Murphy bed.

If you view your home as an arrangement of areas, you would have sleeping, bathing, dressing, eating, sitting, playing, and working areas. Because you can group these areas conceptually into private, semiprivate, and public, you can arrange and treat them accordingly.

The area around the main door is the most public. This is followed, most commonly, by the living room and dining room. Then comes the family room, followed by the bedrooms and bathrooms. A home office will be more or less public or private.

Using common sense, you can create a graduated treatment of these areas to emphasize their public and private functions by implementing one or more of the following suggestions:

- Use more formal furniture arrangements in the more public areas and less formal to completely informal furniture arrangements in the more private areas.
- Use fewer, smaller, or thinner floor coverings in the public areas and more, larger, or thicker floor coverings in the private areas.
- Use less or thinner drapery in the public areas and more or thicker drapery in the private areas.
- Use harder wall textures in the more public areas and softer wall textures in the bedroom especially.

You might also want to consider these ideas:

- Higher ceilings and larger rooms inspire formality and greater distance between people, while lower ceilings and smaller rooms inspire greater intimacy.
- Diffused lighting moves people apart, while localized lighting brings people together. You can easily manipulate the play of light and shadow in your home to create pools of light and imaginary pathways.
- Always decorate your home with what is meaningful to you. Trust your feelings. Let your home evolve over time. If you are a creative artist, you know that your best and most meaningful works come from the deepest levels of your being; they are authentic expressions of your process in life. The same should hold true for how you decorate your home. Don't let the dictates of fashion overrule your personal taste. The warmest, most beautiful homes always display the naturally evolving personalities and histories of their occupants. It is far more pleasurable and comforting to come into a home that is decorated with things that have real personal meaning to its occupants than to come into a home that has been decorated to look like a fashion plate. If you want your home to attract love, take a loving interest in all that is part of your life. Decorate your home with things related to your life

and things that attract you, such as personally meaningful paintings, drawings, carvings, old family photographs, and so forth. Make the space your own. Let your natural instincts dictate your choices.

Choosing the Best Room for Your Bedroom

Contrary to contemporary taste, the master bedroom does not have to be the largest room in the house, replete with entertainment unit, open bath, and panoramic views. Considering how the bedroom by its very nature is a most intimate place and is used, among other things, for sleeping, its position should be determined according to the following guidelines:

- The bedroom should be in a more or less secluded area of your home. Its door should not be visible from the main door of your home. If it is, put a full-length mirror on the outside of the bedroom door and keep the door closed to deflect the chi coming in from outside.
- Depending on when you normally wake up, your bedroom should be positioned so the sunlight will come in at that time. For example, if you wake up early in the morning, your bedroom ideally should have windows that look to the east and southeast if you live in the Northern Hemisphere or to the east and northeast if you live in the Southern Hemisphere.
- It is always good to choose a room in which you can align your bed to your relationship element or, if you are a couple, to your element of mutual harmony. We will discuss this in full detail in Chapter 10.
- The size of the bedroom is not nearly as important as the quality of its chi. You can determine the most positive areas of your home either by taking note of how you feel in the different rooms and areas or by applying the following compass method to your floor plan.

If your main door faces **north,** the most positive levels of chi are in the north, east, southeast, and south areas of your home, as shown in figure 11.

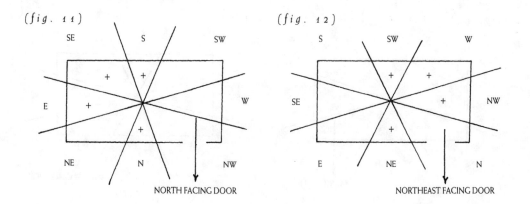

(fig. 11)

NORTH FACING DOOR

(fig. 12)

NORTHEAST FACING DOOR

If your main door faces **northeast**, the most positive levels of chi are in the northeast, southwest, west, and northwest areas of your home, as shown in figure 12.

If your main door faces **east**, the most positive levels of chi are in the east, southeast, south, and north areas of your home, as shown in figure 13.

If your main door faces **southeast**, the most positive levels of chi are in the southeast, south, north, and east areas of your home, as shown in figure 14.

If your main door faces **south**, the most positive levels of chi are in the south, north, east, and southeast areas of your home, as shown in figure 15.

If your main door faces **southwest**, the most positive levels of chi are in the southwest, west, northwest, and northeast areas of your home, as shown in figure 16.

If your main door faces **west**, the most positive levels of chi are in the west, northwest, northeast, and southwest areas of your home, as shown in figure 17.

If your main door faces **northwest**, the most positive levels of chi are in the northwest, northeast, southwest, and west areas of your home, as shown in figure 18.

If you find that you can't use one of these positive areas for your bedroom, don't worry. In Chapter 15 I will show you how to change the negative levels of chi to positive.

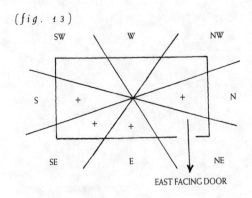

(fig. 13)

EAST FACING DOOR

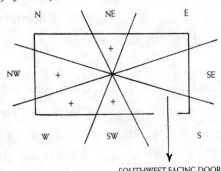

(fig. 14)

SOUTHEAST FACING DOOR

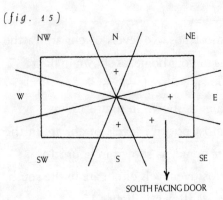

(fig. 15)

SOUTH FACING DOOR

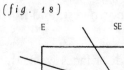

(fig. 16)

SOUTHWEST FACING DOOR

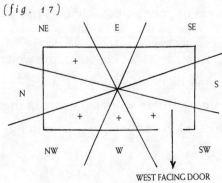

(fig. 17)

WEST FACING DOOR

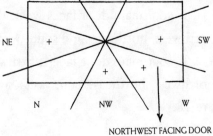

(fig. 18)

NORTHWEST FACING DOOR

Choosing the Best Room for Your Area of Special Interest

If your special interest requires a special room or area in which to work, try to keep it separate from the more social areas, and definitely away from your bedroom. If you want to have a fulfilling love relationship, take all your work, including your computer, desk, file cabinets, papers, and so forth, out of your bedroom.

If you live in a one-bedroom apartment, divide the living room and use half of it for your work. Or if you don't need so much room, create a smaller but separate space, away from the social-entertainment area, where you can keep your work undisturbed. If you live in a studio apartment, try to make discrete areas in it for sleeping, living, and working.

If the room you want to use for your special interest is in an unrelated compass area of your home, or if you don't want to pursue your special interest at home, choose a wall in its corresponding compass direction and decorate it with appropriate pictures or symbolic objects or cut out Talisman 3 from the back of this book, mount and frame it, and hang it there. For example, if the compass direction that corresponds to your area of special interest is north, choose a wall in the north section of your home or in the north area of a particular room, such as your living room or home office, to display Talisman 3.

When You Live Together

When two people live together, it is very important for them to accommodate each other's tastes. If you arrange your home without considering each other's preferences, one or both of you will eventually feel out of place and discontented. For a home to be well-balanced, it must have separate areas to accommodate the unique individuals who live there. Even if your home is small, it is possible to create private areas, like alcoves or nooks, to accommodate your unique personalities and common areas to accommodate your togetherness.

Exercises

- Locate the yin and yang areas of your home. Is your bedroom, or bed, in a yin area? Is the living room in a yang area? If your bedroom is in a yang area, you can soften its chi by using subdued colors. If your living room is in a yin area, you can raise its chi by using brighter colors.

- Mark the public, semiprivate, and private function of each room or area of your home on your floor plan. Try to envision a progression of furniture arrangements and treatments among these areas using some of the ideas suggested in this chapter.

- Mark the areas of positive chi on your floor plan, as delineated in figures 11 through 18.

chapter 9

The Main Door

In feng shui the two most important things to consider are the situation of the main door and the alignment of the bed. The main door, in various ways, conditions the chi of your entire home. Because it is a cross point, it determines the conditions in which you live not only by virtue of the element corresponding to its compass direction but by what it causes you to see when looking in as well as out.

Ideally, the entrance to your home should offer you a pleasant transition between the world outside and the quieter world inside. It should be arranged simply and be free from clutter so that movement in and out feels easy. If your entrance area is roomy enough, you can keep a vase of fresh flowers or fountain in it, in addition to pleasant pictures, to add a touch of freshness and ease to your home.

The Main Door in Relation to the Inside of Your Home

What you see upon first entering very much influences the way you feel about your home. It is best to come into a comfortable foyer or entrance hall, with the more public rooms off to the sides and the more private rooms completely out of sight.

- If your main door opens directly into your living room, or any room for that matter, the room will be too exposed to what is outside, and the space around the doorway will be more or less useless. To remedy this, place a bench, standing plants, and/or cabinetry near the doorway to create the feeling of an entrance area. If you live in a studio apartment that has no entrance hall or foyer, try to place attractive storage units near the door. Be careful, however, not to obstruct or crowd the doorway.

- It is considered bad feng shui if, upon opening the main door, you can see a bathroom door or bedroom door. To remedy this condition, attach a full-length mirror on the outside of the bathroom or bedroom door, and always keep the door shut.

- If upon opening the main door you see directly into the kitchen, especially if it is a galley kitchen in an apartment, keep the kitchen door closed or, if you don't want to keep the door closed or there isn't a kitchen door, hang a Japanese curtain door, or beaded curtain, at the kitchen entrance to give it a sense of privacy. If, however, your main door opens directly into a large kitchen and dining area, be sure to make it a warm and inviting room.

- The doorway should not face a corner, as shown in figure 19. If it does, put a mirror or decorative object on the extended area of the wall, as shown by figure 20.

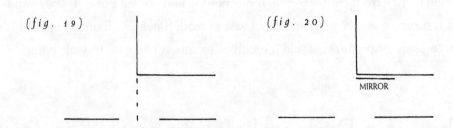

(fig. 19)   *(fig. 20)*

MIRROR

- The entryway should not be cramped. If your main door opens into a tight space, hang a small, attractive picture on the wall facing the door.

- The doorway should not directly face a freestanding structural column. If it does, put an attractive standing plant in front of the column to camouflage it or attach full-length mirrors to all sides of the column.

- It is considered bad feng shui for the main door to be directly in line with, and within view of, the back door. If you have this situation, screen off the back door so that it is not visible from the main door.

The Main Door in Relation to What Is Outside

As important as it is to look inside to detect trouble spots, it is also important to look outside.

- The main door should not face a road or driveway that runs directly toward or away from it, as shown in figure 21.

(fig. 21)

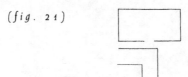

- The main door should not face a U-shaped road or overpass, called a curved blade, as shown in figure 22.

(fig. 22)

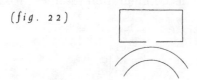

- The main door should not directly face the end of a cul-de-sac or T-junction, as shown in figure 23.

(fig. 23)

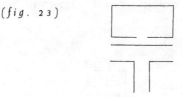

- The main door should not face a building situated at an angle, as shown in figure 24.

(fig. 24)

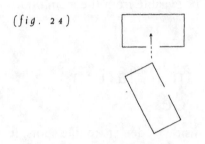

- The main door should not face any sharp objects pointing directly at it.
- The main door should not face a dead tree or building that is falling into ruin.
- The main door should not face part of another building and part of an empty lot, as shown in figure 25.

(fig. 25)

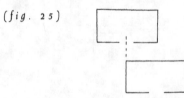

- The main door should not face two buildings separated by a narrow alley, as shown in figure 26. This configuration signifies broken luck.

(fig. 26)

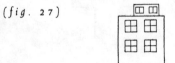

- The main door should not face two buildings in which the one in back rises slightly higher than the one in front, as shown in figure 27. This configuration denotes theft.

(fig. 27)

- The main door should not face a single building that towers over all its neighbors. Such a building presages fighting.
- You should not be able to see water towers on top of neighboring buildings from your main door. They are called tigers' heads and presage loss of money.
- The main door should not face suspended electrical or telephone wires, or train tracks that are either elevated or running along the ground.
- The main door should not face smokestacks.
- The main door should not face a power plant, sewage plant, garbage dump, police station, firehouse, jail, hospital, funeral parlor, gambling hall, or anything that makes you feel uneasy.

Remedies by Compass Direction

If your doorway faces any of these problematic conditions, put plants, such as evergreen shrubs, at the sides of the doorway, as shown in figure 28, hang bells or wind chimes in the entryway, and/or use colors as follows:

(*fig.* 2 8)

- If your doorway faces **north**, put something green or light blue at the door.
- If your doorway faces **northeast**, put something white, gray, or silver at the door.
- If your doorway faces **east**, put something red, purple, rose, or pink at the door.
- If your doorway faces **southeast**, put something red, purple, rose, or pink at the door.
- If your doorway faces **south**, put something yellow, gold, orange, brown, tan, or beige at the door.
- If your doorway faces **southwest**, put something white, gray, or silver at the door.
- If your doorway faces **west**, put something black or deep blue at the door.
- If your doorway faces **northwest**, put something black or deep blue at the door.

What you put at the door can be a picture, a wreath, some other decorative object, or a floor mat that is predominantly the color you need. It does not have to be large. You can place a decorative object to the side, on, or above the door. Always use common sense and good taste in your choices.

The Main Door Opening to a Corridor

When you live in an apartment building, the door to your apartment should not directly face your neighbor's door across the hall. Neither should it directly face a stairwell, an elevator, or a corner, as was shown in figure 19. If your doorway faces any of these trouble spots, hang bells or wind chimes in your entryway and/or use the colors just described.

Your Door Fortune

While your fate is not necessarily sealed by the door of your home, the door does make some subtle hints about your prospects. Your door fortune is derived from the combination of your personal element (the element of your day of birth) and the element that corresponds to your door's compass direction.

In the table of yin-yang personal element and door direction combinations, you will find the number that indicates your door fortune where your yin-yang personal element meets your door direction. For example, if your yin-yang personal element is yin Earth and your door looks out to the north, you would read paragraph 9 in the fortunes. Or if your yin-yang personal element is yang Metal and your door direction is south, you would read paragraph 37.

Please note, the yin-yang qualities for the elements Water and Fire appear together in this system, while the yin and yang qualities for the other elements appear separately.

Yin-Yang Personal Element and Door Direction Combinations

		Yin-Yang	Yin	Yang	Yin	Yang	Yin	Yang	Yin-Yang
Yin-Yang Personal Element		Water	Earth	Wood	Wood	Metal	Metal	Earth	Fire
Door Directions	North	1	9	17	25	33	41	49	57
	Northeast	2	10	18	26	34	42	50	58
	East	3	11	19	27	35	43	51	59
	Southeast	4	12	20	28	36	44	52	60
	South	5	13	21	29	37	45	53	61
	Southwest	6	14	22	30	38	46	54	62
	West	7	15	23	31	39	47	55	63
	Northwest	8	16	24	32	40	48	56	64

Door Fortunes

1. Be cautious when accepting proposals and making commitments. When experiencing difficulties, don't try to force matters. Changes for the better come in due course.

2. Be modest about what you want. You will be at a disadvantage if you expect too much. Exercise wisdom in choosing your partner and in making commitments. Unless you pay attention to details and work things out carefully, your relationship may lose all sense of direction.

3. Carpe diem! Conditions are favorable for love and marriage. If you hesitate too long to make commitments, however, you may lose your chances for success.

4. All will go well if you don't rush. Whatever you want will come in time. Don't overlook details. Guard against unwanted intrusions and interferences.

5. The future looks bright. However, proceed step by step. The conditions are excellent for marriage.

6. Good fortune comes with experience. If you and your partner fight, either settle it once and for all or move on. If you learn from your mistakes, you inevitably will be happy.

7. If you are having trouble in your relationship, a trusted third party will help you resolve your differences so that the relationship will work. Avoid causing unnecessary trouble. Self-indulgence and irresponsibility will bear a price.

8. If you are impatient, you may fall into untoward circumstances from which it will be difficult to extricate yourself. If you are modest and flexible, all will turn out satisfactorily. Forcing matters bodes ill. Avoid love triangles.

9. The conditions are excellent for marriage and all joint ventures. Don't doubt your good fortune. If you hesitate too long to make commitments, you may lose your opportunities.

10. Beware of those who would take unfair advantage of you. If you are naive in your expectations, you may run into unexpected difficulties in your relationship. However, if you are realistic about your partner, you can look forward to much happiness.

11. Carpe diem! If you take positive and timely actions, you can look forward to much joy. If you stay focused and pursue your aims in an orderly way, you will be successful.

12. If there is too great a difference between your wishes and reality, you will fail to recognize your opportunities. Be down to earth. Aiming too high will overshoot the mark.

13. The conditions are favorable for love and marriage. Your luck is strong. However, don't press it and ruin your opportunities. Beware of attracting envy.

14. Conditions for love and marriage are ideal. Cooperation with others will bring great happiness. Avoid being impatient. Everything you want will happen in due time.

15. While your chances for happiness in love and marriage are good, the more you hesitate to take positive and timely actions, the more you will be allowing undesirable conditions to develop. If interferences or other difficulties in your relationship develop, a neutral third party will be able to help you.

16. Be patient in troubled times. Everything changes. Difficult conditions eventually change for the better. If you view problems in your relationship with an open mind and are willing to make reasonable compromises, you can look forward to much happiness.

17. When prevailing circumstances prevent you from carrying out your intentions, be patient and wait for conditions to change. Trying to force matters will do more harm than good. While ultimately you will be successful, don't be surprised if progress is slow.

18. Be careful about what you say. Inconsiderate words and lies will cause you a lot of trouble. If you are having a lovers' quarrel, be patient. Don't overreact. The indications for love and marriage are good, providing both you and your partner are realistic.

19. Avoid causing rivalries. The more jealous you are, the poorer your sense of judgment. If you make commitments or marry impulsively, you may be in for a rude awakening. If you are levelheaded, however, you can look forward to great happiness.

20. The indications for a fortunate marriage are excellent. You will be especially fortunate if you are compassionate and patient. You may fall in love at first sight. However, give ample time to developing your relationship.

21. Act resolutely to remove obstacles when they appear. Beware of troubles that may come up between you and your partner because of the interference of others. Letting others interfere with your relationship will result in misfortune.

22. Difficult times are followed by easy times. In times of difficulty, be patient and optimistic. If you act impulsively you will ruin your luck. You will be fortunate in love if you take your time.

23. Although the indications for love and marriage are excellent, exercise clear judgment, and avoid those whose intentions are suspect. When in doubt seek the advice of an older and trustworthy person.

24. If you are anxious about your relationship, relax and let it take a natural course. If you act impatiently you will only complicate matters. Avoid unnecessary quarrels. You will succeed if you go with the flow.

25. Conditions are uneven. While you definitely will make progress, there will be reversals. Kind words and good deeds will ensure the ultimate success of your relationship. Relax and bide your time without harboring resentments when conditions seem unfavorable.

26. Beware of misplaced affections. Work on yourself to overcome your inner

conflicts and confusion. When under pressure, be patient. Impatience will lead to misfortune. Avoid unwanted complications in your love life. If you approach your relationships with a level head, you will find happiness.

27. If you ignore your loved one's needs because of your conflicting interests, don't be surprised when he or she loses patience with you and breaks off the relationship. If you want your relationship to succeed, be considerate and flexible.

28. If you are unsure of yourself and prone to changing your mind again and again, your love life will become overly complicated. Too much shilly-shallying will result in loss. Contentment is the greatest wealth.

29. The indications for love and marriage are excellent, especially if you take the lead. Be careful about triangles, however. You will be most fortunate when you have completely resolved old affairs and are free to move forward.

30. The indications for love and marriage are excellent. Take advantage of your opportunities and cultivate your ability to adapt in order to move around obstacles. Small steps will take you most directly to your goal.

31. It pays to exercise self-restraint. Going to extremes and forcing matters will cause misfortune. If conditions become too complicated and burdensome, stay calm and wait cautiously for things to change for the better.

32. Be alert. Entertaining relations with people whose intentions are dishonest will only bring misfortune. If you cultivate yourself, however, those who are good and destined to be with you will appear.

33. Although the indications for love and marriage are good, don't rush into any-thing. You may have to wait a long time to have what you want. If unexpected help comes to you, don't turn it down.

34. While the indications for love and marriage are excellent, you will not attain what you want without some difficulty. When confronted with obstacles bide your time. Avoid unnecessary arguments. The way will open for you naturally.

35. Trying to get your way by using force will bring misfortune. While it is good to persevere, avoid using power. If you are flexible and adaptable, the way will open for you to attain what you desire.

36. If obstacles to your happiness appear slight, attempting to force your way against them will have undesirable consequences. It is best to cultivate

gentleness and sincerity toward others. Then your obstacles will give way naturally.

37. The prospects for marriage are excellent, especially if you are in the lead. You will have success if you are open, generous, and forthright in your actions. If you are in the passive role, avoid impatience.

38. The indications for love and marriage are excellent. Strive to bring all the elements of your life and relationship into great harmony. If you presume upon your good fortune, you will experience a decline.

39. Don't go overboard for someone who is not willing to meet you halfway. If you are having trouble with your mate, stop acting out of passion and turn to reason. Seek a middle course. Carelessness will lead to misfortune.

40. You will be most successful when you conquer all your doubts and act creatively. If your aspirations exceed your power, however, or if you are courting someone who cannot make or keep commitments, you will reach an impasse. Be flexible. Know when to advance and when to retreat.

41. Good fortune lies in knowing exactly when to act and when not to act. Saying too much and saying too little are both unfortunate. Find the middle way. If you are not overly anxious to marry or make commitments, you will be most fortunate.

42. The more you give, the more you will receive. The less selfish you are, the more you will attract love. Avoid triangles. If you are content when alone, you will find your destined companion. Your relationship will be successful if you don't rush it.

43. Be absolutely certain of your intentions. Acting on whims bodes ill. If you intend to marry or make deep commitments, proceed with caution. If you start out on the wrong foot, you will fall into trouble.

44. The indications for love and marriage are excellent. You will attain whatever you want as long as you act. Words alone will accomplish nothing. Be liberal toward others while unwaveringly pursuing your aims. Boasting bodes ill.

45. In times of opposition and misunderstanding, remain firm and adhere to your principles. Be clear about your loyalties and commitments. Avoid becoming embroiled in useless conflicts. Interferences and obstacles to your relationship will pass in time. If you are meant to be together, you both will triumph.

46. The outlook for love and marriage is excellent. Everything favors strong progress and success. Difficulties if they arise can be overcome easily. Take full advantage of your opportunities. When in doubt, you can rely on the helpful advice of an older woman.

47. While the indications for love and marriage are good, the empty pursuit of pleasure will bring misfortune. Your degree of inner harmony and stability will be reflected in the depth of joy and understanding in your relationship.

48. If you are resolute and circumspect, you will attain your wishes. Be certain of every move you make. If you act impulsively or overreach yourself, you will fall into trouble. Pay attention to details.

49. Be content with your situation. If you are beset by obstacles welcome the help of friends. But also be willing to assist others. That way you will be fortunate.

50. Find the way to be at peace with your situation. Working at inner balance and harmony will give you the patience to wait for appropriate opportunities. Impatient or impulsive moves will lead to misfortune.

51. You will do well to be considerate of others and conservative in your actions. Pay attention to details. If you make commitments you cannot keep, you will be courting disaster. Impatience will lead to misfortune.

52. The outlook for love and marriage is excellent. Let matters develop quietly and naturally. If you try to force results, however, you will be provoking conflict. What is meant to be will be. Have good faith.

53. If you are restless and discontented with your lot, your love life will suffer. Don't be dazzled by glamorous opportunities. Examine them carefully; they may turn out to be empty. Carelessness and lack of consideration for your partner's feelings will lead to misfortune.

54. The outlook for love and marriage depends on how moderate and simple you are. Self-discipline and modesty will win the goodwill and love of others.

55. The prospects for love and marriage are excellent. What you wish for will come true if you hold your intention and are patient. If, however, you are doubtful, prone to changing your mind over and over again, and too talkative, you will undermine your luck.

56. Retreat. Whoever is meant to be with you will be with you. Keep envious and

quarrelsome people at arm's length. Inner detachment and self-reliance will bring good fortune.

57. While the outlook for love and marriage is good, don't take your relationship for granted. If you let a careless attitude set in, your relationship will deteriorate. The best way for your relationship to remain vital and happy is for you to undertake an appropriate spiritual path together.

58. Love will go well for you as long as you deal with it simply and honestly. Be forthright and truthful with others. Glamorous pretense will lead to misfortune.

59. The prospects for love and marriage are good. However, beware of intrigues and petty arguments that can undermine your happiness. Be patient and generous toward your loved one.

60. The indications for marriage are excellent. It is essential, however, that you agree on a definite order to your relationship and arrangement of domestic affairs. When you achieve a state of contentment, you will enjoy great good fortune.

61. You will be fortunate in love if you find the middle way. Be content with what is natural and normal. If you are not at peace with life, you will meet with misfortune. Practice self-restraint.

62. If you wish to be fortunate in love, it is essential that you recognize the subtle roots of adverse conditions that may arise and avoid tangling with them. If trouble does arise remain upright and alert, but don't try to set things straight too quickly. Let it pass naturally.

63. Wherever you are discontented in your life, make revolutionary changes. If your relationship is becoming stagnant, renew it. Carefully consider your course of action before doing anything. Affecting revolutionary changes when needed will bring great good fortune.

64. Your relationship will be most successful if you let it develop gradually and naturally. Considering how all things in the universe are interdependent, cultivate harmonious and healthy relations with everyone around you to ensure the smooth progress of your love relationship. If you encounter obstacles remember, if your relationship is good nothing will be able to keep you apart for long.

Exercises

- If you haven't already done so, stand at the main door to your home and look in. If you find any of the trouble spots listed in this chapter, enter them along with their appropriate solutions in your Things to Do list.

- Stand at the main door to your home and look out. If you find any of the trouble spots listed in this chapter, enter them along with their appropriate solutions in your Things to Do list.

- If your door fortune implies problematic conditions for you, cut out Talisman 4 from the back of this book, mount and frame it, and hang it by your doorway to neutralize any negative meanings and bring a spirit of protection to your home.

chapter 10

The Bedroom and Bath

In arranging your bedroom, the first and most important thing to decide is where to put your bed. Because there are several things to consider, the placement of the bed may require weighing various factors and making compensatory adjustments. Not only does the bed have to be positioned in a correct relation to the bedroom door and windows but it has to be aligned to a direction that is in harmony with your astrological element. Let's look at these details in order.

Placing Your Bed in Relation to Door and Windows

Several bed placements don't work well and should be avoided if at all possible. They are as follows:

- Do not put the bed where its foot points directly out the door, as shown in figure 29. If you have no other choice, hang a curtain over the doorframe to screen the doorway when you are sleeping.

(fig. 29)

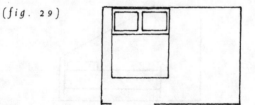

- Do not put the bed in line with the path of chi coming in from the door-way, as shown in figure 30. If you have no other choice, hang a curtain over the doorframe to screen the doorway when you are sleeping.

(fig. 30)

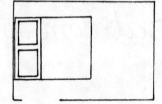

- Do not put the bed where its foot points directly out a window, as shown in figure 31. If you have no other choice, always keep the window covered when sleeping.

(fig. 31)

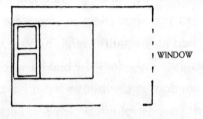

- Do not put the bed directly under a window, as shown in figure 32.

(fig. 32)

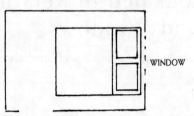

- Do not position the bed under an eaves or sloping ceiling, as shown in figure 33.

(fig. 33)

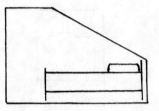

- Do not position the bed where you can get in and out of it on only one side, as shown in figures 34 and 35, unless you intend to live alone. The space between the side of the bed and the wall should be no less than 2 feet. If you cannot get in and out comfortably on both sides, intolerable conditions will inevitably develop in your relationship.

(fig. 34)   *(fig. 35)*

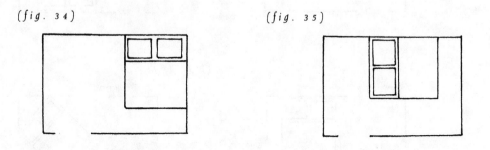

- Do not put the bed under a skylight or where anything is hanging overhead.
- Try to avoid putting your bed against a wall abutting a bathroom. You should not sleep with water pipes behind your head.
- Try to avoid putting your bed against a wall abutting an elevator shaft. You should not sleep with an elevator shaft behind your head.
- It is rumored in feng shui circles that one should never place a bed under exposed beams. This idea probably comes from South China, where there are many severe earthquakes. China is in the Northern Hemisphere, and earthquakes in the Northern Hemisphere almost always happen around sunup, when most people are still asleep. It would stand to reason, therefore, that if you were in bed under a beam during an earthquake, you would be in serious danger. In places where earthquakes don't happen, it doesn't matter if you sleep under a beam or not. If it bothers your aesthetic sense to sleep in a room whose ceiling has exposed beams, either align the bed so that the beams run along the bed's length or have a new ceiling constructed to cover the beams.

Figures 36 through 40 show good placements for a bed. Note how none of them conflicts with the doorway or windows.

Placing the bed catercorner works only if the room is large. Such bed placements take up a lot more space than placements with the head against the wall.

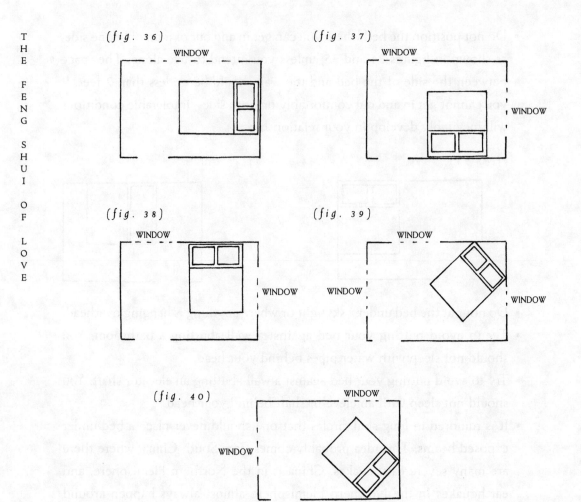

(fig. 36)   (fig. 37)

(fig. 38)   (fig. 39)

(fig. 40)

Positioning Your Bed According to Your Astrological Element

In examining your bedroom for workable bed placements, you may have discovered that you have more than one possibility. The following compass information can help you to narrow down your choices. If you find that you can't align your bed to an appropriate compass direction, don't worry. I will show you what to do about that a little further on.

If you live alone the astrological element to use is your relationship element. If you live as a couple the astrological element to use is one of your elements of mutual harmony.

- If your relationship element or element of mutual harmony is Water, the compass direction toward which to align your bed is north.
- If your relationship element or element of mutual harmony is Wood, the compass directions toward which to align your bed are east or southeast.
- If your relationship element or element of mutual harmony is Fire, the compass direction toward which to align your bed is south.
- If your relationship element or element of mutual harmony is Earth, the compass directions toward which to align your bed are northeast or southwest.
- If your relationship element or element of mutual harmony is Metal, the compass directions toward which to align your bed are west or northwest.

If you are unsure about how to align your bed, please refer back to the instructions in How to Use Part Two.

When You Cannot Align the Bed to Your Astrological Element

Because compass directions and colors both correspond to the elements (Water, Wood, Fire, Earth, Metal), you can use colors to make up for any alignment of your bed that is out of agreement with your astrological element. To do the following color applications, first decide on the placement of your bed according to its relation to your bedroom door and windows, then take the compass reading of its placement.

The colors recommended here can be applied in any number of ways, from your bedspread, carpets, and curtains to your bedroom walls. Because we will be dealing with the entire color scheme of your home in Chapter 15, just make a note of the colors recommended here in your Things to Do list.

- If your bed is aligned to the north but your astrological element is Wood, use greens or light blues on or around your bed.
- If your bed is aligned to the north but your astrological element is Fire, use a combination of greens or light blues with reds, purples, roses, or pinks on or around your bed.

163

- If your bed is aligned to the north but your astrological element is Earth, use a combination of reds, purples, roses, or pinks with yellows, golds, oranges, browns, tans, or beiges on or around your bed.

- If your bed is aligned to the north but your astrological element is Metal, use a combination of yellows, golds, oranges, browns, tans, or beiges with whites, grays, or silver on or around your bed.

- If your bed is aligned to the east or southeast but your astrological element is Fire, use reds, purples, roses, or pinks on or around your bed.

- If your bed is aligned to the east or southeast but your astrological element is Earth, use a combination of reds, purples, roses, or pinks with yellows, golds, oranges, browns, tans, or beiges on or around your bed.

- If your bed is aligned to the east or southeast but your astrological element is Metal, use a combination of yellows, golds, oranges, browns, tans, or beiges with whites, grays, or silver on or around your bed.

- If your bed is aligned to the east or southeast but your astrological element is Water, use a combination of whites, grays, or silver with black or deep blues on or around your bed.

- If your bed is aligned to the south but your astrological element is Earth, use yellows, golds, oranges, browns, tans, or beiges on or around your bed.

- If your bed is aligned to the south but your astrological element is Metal, use a combination of yellows, golds, oranges, browns, tans, or beiges with whites, grays, or silver on or around your bed.

- If your bed is aligned to the south but your astrological element is Water, use a combination of whites, grays, or silver with black or deep blues on or around your bed.

- If your bed is aligned to the south but your astrological element is Wood, use a combination of black or deep blues with greens or light blues on or around your bed.

- If your bed is aligned to the northeast or southwest but your astrological element is Metal, use whites, grays, or silver on or around your bed.

- If your bed is aligned to the northeast or southwest but your astrological element is Water, use a combination of whites, grays, or silver with black or deep blues on or around your bed.
- If your bed is aligned to the northeast or southwest but your astrological element is Wood, use a combination of black or deep blues with greens or light blues on or around your bed.
- If your bed is aligned to the northeast or southwest but your astrological element is Fire, use a combination of greens or light blues with reds, purples, roses, or pinks on or around your bed.

- If your bed is aligned to the west or northwest but your astrological element is Water, use black or deep blues on or around your bed.
- If your bed is aligned to the west or northwest but your astrological element is Wood, use a combination of black or dark blues with greens or light blues on or around your bed.
- If your bed is aligned to the west or northwest but your astrological element is Fire, use a combination of greens or light blues with reds, purples, roses, or pinks on or around your bed.
- If your bed is aligned to the west or northwest but your astrological element is Earth, use a combination of reds, purples, roses, or pinks with yellows, golds, oranges, browns, tans, or beiges on or around your bed.

The following vignettes will demonstrate how these colors can be applied.

Stacy

Stacy lives alone. She was born on April 1st, 1966. Because her style of relating is yang and her personal element is Metal, her relationship element is Wood. For Stacy to align her bed to the element Wood, she would have to position it with its head to the east or southeast. However, the layout of her bedroom lets her place her bed only at the northeast wall. Referring to the paragraph dealing with the color combinations for a bed aligned to the northeast with the astrological element Wood, Stacy chooses a bedspread whose colors include shades of deep blue and light blue.

David and Karen

David and Karen live together. Because David's personal element is Metal and Karen's personal element is Wood, their element of mutual harmony is Water. This means that they should align their bed to the north. Their bedroom, however, will allow them to put the bed only at either the southwest or the northwest wall. They choose to put the bed at the northwest wall. After reading the paragraph dealing with a bed aligned to the northwest and the astrological element Water, they decide to paint the bedroom white, hang white curtains at the windows, put a light gray rug on the floor, and cover the bed with an elegant black-and-white bedspread.

Positioning Other Bedroom Furniture

Position your other pieces of bedroom furniture to form a harmonious and graceful composition with the bed. Depending on the size of your bedroom, you can include pieces such as nightstands, a dresser, an armoire, a chest, a writing table, a couple of comfortable chairs, a chaise longue, or a love seat. Avoid cluttering the room with too much furniture, however. The less freedom you have moving around the room, the less inviting it will be.

Do not position a piece of furniture so that one of its corners points directly at you when you are lying in bed. Objects that point at you can cause irritable feelings.

Use common sense when arranging your bedroom. Let your furniture follow the line of the walls. Never obstruct a window.

It is best not to have a television in the bedroom. Sleeping with the television on or spending a lot of time watching it before going to sleep can drain your vital chi and cause you to become depressed. If you insist on having a television in your bedroom, keep it in a cabinet with doors that you can shut before going to sleep.

Do not keep an aquarium in your bedroom. Besides its distraction, an aquarium has an extremely yin quality that will unbalance the chi of the room and make it feel strangely cold and uncomfortable.

How and How Not to Use Mirrors

The fewer mirrors in the bedroom the better. Mirrors activate chi, and the chi of the bedroom should be as calm as possible.

The worst place to put a mirror is where you can see your reflection when you are lying in bed. If you have a wall unit or armoire with mirrored doors, don't place it at the foot of the bed. Mirrors positioned that way not only oppose your rest but hint at intrusions in your relationship.

Don't hang a mirror on a wall directly opposite a window; it will activate the chi too much. If you must hang a mirror opposite a window, cover the window. Lace or sheer curtains will suffice.

It is not a good idea to hang a mirror or picture on the wall above the head of the bed. If you do, be certain that it is securely fastened to the wall. Anything hanging over your head will contribute to feelings of insecurity and restlessness.

The best places for bedroom mirrors are in intimate areas away from the bed. Such places may include a dressing area or a vanity. An ornamental mirror placed in such a way that it is partially hidden by a standing plant can create a romantic effect. An ornamental mirror hung near the entrance of your bedroom is also fine.

Symbolic Decorations

Once you have a basic idea about how you want to arrange your furniture, you can begin to think about how to decorate your bedroom. Several approaches deserve consideration:

- Because the bedroom is the most informal area of your home, try to avoid arranging and decorating it with too much symmetry. It is not necessary to hang pictures precisely at the centers of the walls or exactly midpoint between the windows, for example. Pictures artfully placed off center can bring a graceful feeling to the room.
- Pictures should relate to the areas you have created with your furniture placements. In other words, hang pictures in a sitting area, by a writing table, and so forth.

- To subtly heighten the romantic atmosphere, use pairs of things. Avoid odd numbers, especially threes. Hang pictures of loving couples; pictures in pairs; two, four, or six pictures of a similar nature; and so on. Put two chairs in a sitting area instead of one or three.

- While you definitely should use pictures and other decorative objects that have personal meaning to you, you can also use any of the following traditional Chinese symbols.

Symbol	Meaning
Pair of lovebirds	Romantic love
Butterflies	Love and joy
Cranes	Fidelity
Ducks	Joy
Wild geese	Conjugal fidelity
Phoenix	Love and peace
Peach	Marriage
Peonies	Love
Pomegranate	Many prosperous offspring
Roses	Beauty and love

- For a truly magical effect, you can hang Talismans 2 and/or 5, found in the back of the book, in the area of your bedroom that corresponds to your relationship element or element of mutual harmony. Otherwise, you can hang one or both of these talismans in the marriage point area of your bedroom. If you frame one of these talismans, first mount it on a mat whose color corresponds to your relationship element or element of mutual harmony. Remember, black or deep blues correspond to Water; greens or light blues correspond to Wood; reds, purples, roses, or pinks correspond to Fire; yellows, golds, oranges, browns, tans, or beiges correspond to Earth; and whites, grays, or silver correspond to Metal.

The Bathroom

In looking at and treating the bathroom, you need to consider where it is and what condition it is in. The following situations are problematic:

- A bathroom in the northeast area of a home attracts illness and decay. If your bathroom is in this area of your home, paint it white and put a full-length mirror on the outside of its door to neutralize its chi.

- A bathroom in the west area is unlucky for women and for romance. If your bathroom is in this area of your home, use combinations of black and green in it. For example, install some black tiles, use green towels, and so forth.

- A bathroom in the center of a house depresses the chi of the entire house. If your bathroom is in the center of your home, attach mirrors to the walls to reflect one another, and put a full-length mirror on the outside of its door to neutralize its chi.

- A bathroom at the marriage point of your home, or in the area corresponding to your relationship element or element of mutual harmony, is not fortunate. If your bathroom is situated in one of these areas, attach a full-length mirror to the outside of its door to neutralize its chi.

- If your bathroom has no windows, treat it as you would a bathroom in the center of your home. The activation of positive chi will compensate for the lack of circulating air. Nonetheless, make sure the ventilation system is in top condition. If it isn't, the air, and therefore the chi, will become all the more stagnant there, even with the mirrors.

- Make sure the plumbing in the bathroom is in good condition. Leaking faucets and defective plumbing, besides contributing to the actual deterioration of your home, hint of luck running out.

Exercises

- Relative to the door and windows of your bedroom, which are the best placements for your bed? Lightly sketch one or more of these placements on a copy of your floor plan.

- If your bedroom allows you to position your bed in more than one area, can you align it to the compass direction of your relationship element or element of mutual harmony? If so, mark that placement on your floor plan.

- If your room does not allow you to align your bed to the compass direction of your relationship element or element of mutual harmony, choose the best position your room allows for your bed, and mark it on your floor plan.

- If your room does not allow you to align your bed to the compass direction of your astrological element (relationship element or element of mutual harmony), what colors can you use to compensate for the difference between the alignment you are going to use and your astrological element? Make note of these colors in the appropriate place on your floor plan and/or your Things to Do list.

- Once you have determined the best possible placement for your bed, sketch the placement of your other articles of bedroom furniture on your floor plan. Be careful to keep the lines of your configurations smooth and simple. There should be no feeling of obstructed movement in the room.

chapter 11

The Kitchen and Dining Area

In most houses built during past centuries, the kitchen was the location of the hearth. It was the largest room in the house and the place where everyone congregated. In a sense the kitchen was the family room. It was also where everyone from the neighborhood could get together. Besides having cupboards, shelves, counter space, a cooking area, and so forth, it contained a large table, plenty of kinds of chairs, and maybe even a couch or bed off to the side. People would gather there to play games, tell stories, and discuss the local news and business, as well as share in the cooking and eating. The hearth was the spiritual center of the home.

During the eighteenth and nineteenth centuries in Western Europe and America, where it became fashionable for the growing middle class to imitate the older aristocracy and use servants, the kitchen, dining room, and living room were made into separate rooms. Instead of being central to the life of the home, the kitchen was relegated to the back of the house, away from family activity and out of the sight of guests.

Considering how the activity of cooking has forever been under the control of women, this isolation and degradation of the kitchen, and the association of cooking with servitude, have had profound consequences. What woman in her right mind enjoys being thought of or treated as a servant?

As long as you live in an apartment or house whose kitchen is isolated, small, and inappropriate to use as a common area, it will remain more or less difficult for you to integrate the business of cooking with family and social activities. What is more essential to life than food? Food *is* life. Because it is shared, its preparation or time of preparation should also be shared.

While some more modern homes in America have their kitchens partly opened to the dining area and family room, they still do not resolve the problem. The kitchen should be an integral part of the common area. Nothing should split them. The kitchen–common area should be a large, warm room where family and friends can gather to share food preparation and experience the pleasures of community.

If you live as a couple or family and are thinking of remodeling your home, looking for a new home, or even building a home, I heartily recommend having a large, open kitchen, like the old-fashioned country kitchen. The least you should go for is a large, comfortable eat-in kitchen with plenty of counter space and windows.

In order for a kitchen to function most efficiently, the stove, sink, refrigerator, cabinets, shelves, and counters should be comfortably positioned in relation to one another. There should be at least 12 feet of counter space altogether, with no one section of the counter less than 4 feet long. If you do not have enough counter space, use a table or large butcher's block.

The relative positions of the stove, sink, and refrigerator are critical. The following configurations are classic problems.

The stove positioned between the refrigerator and sink, as shown in figure 41; or opposite the sink and refrigerator, as shown in figure 42; or on an island, as shown by figure 43, presages discontentment and quarreling between husband and

(fig. 41)

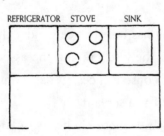

(fig. 42)

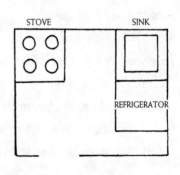

wife. The refrigerator, sink, and stove in a line as shown in figure 44 presages confusion and lack of perspective in life.

(fig. 43)

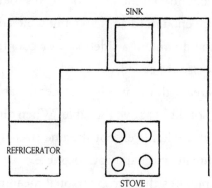

(fig. 44)

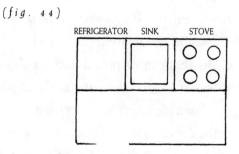

To neutralize the conflict and confusion presaged by these configurations, introduce greens or light blues. In an arrangement resembling either figure 41 or 44, put something green or light blue on the wall above the stove and sink. For example, you can attach a special ornament or configuration of tiles to the wall. In an arrangement resembling either figure 42 or 43, place a green or blue floor mat between the stove and other appliances, or cover the entire floor with linoleum or tiles containing green or light blue.

The stove should not be placed too close to a door or in the way of normal traffic. Neither should it be where the ventilation and lighting are poor, or under a window or skylight.

A door directly behind the stove, as shown in figure 45, can make you feel insecure when cooking. If you cannot move the stove to a better place, put a mirror up somewhere near the stove so that you can see what's going on behind you when you are standing there.

(fig. 45)

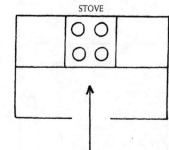

The Dining Area

Whether you have a dining room, a dining area in your living room or studio apartment, or a dining area in the sort of large country kitchen I advocate, it should be a warm and inviting place. It should be large enough to contain a big table and chairs that can be pulled back easily, and should contain a sideboard or counter space for food, dishes, utensils, and whatever else is needed.

For a pleasant effect, decorate the dining area with warm colors, place the table in the center of the area, and hang a beautiful, soft light above the table. When dining with loved ones and friends, turn down all the lights except the one over the table. It will draw everyone together in an intimate and happy atmosphere.

Decorate the dining area with cheerful pictures that have personal meaning to you. If you like, you can use any of the symbolic images listed on page 168.

As in the bedroom, hang pictures in pairs. They don't have to be two of the same, but they should be pairs of similar character. For example, you could hang two pictures of similar scenes, two pictures of flowers such as roses and peonies, two obviously romantic pictures, and so forth.

You should also have an even number of chairs at the table. Even numbers suggest pairs, and pairs suggest loving couples. As an old Chinese proverb says, "Happiness comes in pairs."

If you live in an apartment that has a dining alcove or dining area in the living room, you will have to do something to make it feel intimate. If you have a dining alcove, such as that shown in figure 46, you can enhance its potential by using screens or standing plants. If your dining area resembles figure 47, you can define it better with the back of a couch, a low-standing cabinet, or another piece of furniture.

(fig. 46)

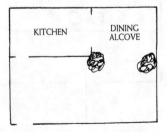

KITCHEN   DINING
ALCOVE

(fig. 47)

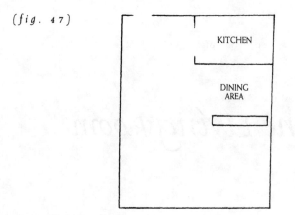

Table shapes have symbolic meanings, some of which are more romantic than others. The most romantic and conducive to love are the round and square. The square means the blessings of earth. The circle means the blessings of heaven. Between the two the round table is the more versatile.

After the round and square comes the octagonal table. The octagon symbolizes the gathering of heaven and earth and all their children. After the octagonal table come the oval and the rectangle. While these two shapes are the most efficient, they suggest hierarchy because they have a head and a foot. Hierarchy implies power, not love.

The worst shape for a table is the triangle. While they are rare, I have seen triangular tables. Because the triangle symbolizes aggression and fighting, it should not be used if you want your home to attract love and peace.

Exercises

- Examine your kitchen for any of the problematic conditions illustrated in figures 41 through 45. If your kitchen resembles any of these, make a note of the appropriate remedy in your Things to Do list.
- Following the suggestions for creating an intimate dining area, sketch your ideas on a copy of your floor plan and make notes in your Things to Do list. How many chairs will you include? What shape table will you choose? What pictures will you use? What warm colors attract you? Please wait until you have read all of Part Two before you settle on any one color, however.

chapter 12

The Living Room

Depending on your taste, your living room can be arranged in either a formal or an informal way. Because it is the most yang and public room in your home, the living room should be inviting and cheerful, and easy to move around in. If your furniture is too large for your room, if you have too much furniture, if it is awkwardly positioned, or if your living room is otherwise cluttered or disorganized, no one will want to stay in it for long.

The simplest and best way to organize your living room is to follow the natural flow of its chi. You can ascertain the flow of chi easily by sketching a line around the room on a copy of your floor plan, beginning at the doorway, as suggested by figure 48.

(*fig. 48*)

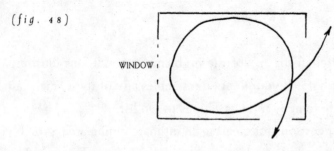

WINDOW

Considering that the chi flows in and out the door and windows, and circulates around the room, arrange your furniture so that it follows the room's contours without interfering with the natural line of traffic. Put the sitting area where it feels most protected, in a configuration that suggests a circle and that embraces the current of chi, as shown in figure 49, so that people will want to come in and sit down.

(fig. 49)

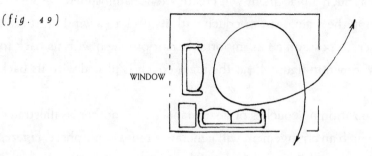

WINDOW

If you have a very large living room, as suggested by figure 50, you can arrange more than one sitting area. If you create two sitting areas, they should be more or less balanced and arranged so that it is easy to move from one to the other.

(fig. 50)

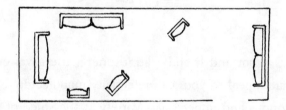

If you need to include your home office in your living room, either select a small area for the office (an alcove would be perfect) or divide the room roughly in half, as suggested by figure 51.

(fig. 51)

BOOKCASES

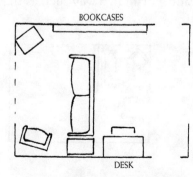

DESK

177

Detailed Guidelines

- Avoid positioning the main chair or couch so that it squarely faces the living room door. Such a placement will create a tense atmosphere.

- Do not position the main chair or couch with its back to a window. It is all right, however, to position a less important chair or couch with its back to a window, as shown in figure 49, if the main couch is placed with its back to a wall.

- Try to avoid positioning couches or chairs facing one another, as illustrated by figure 52. Such an arrangement will generate a tense atmosphere. Figures 53 and 54 show more relaxed and friendlier arrangements.

(fig. 52)   (fig. 53)   (fig. 54)

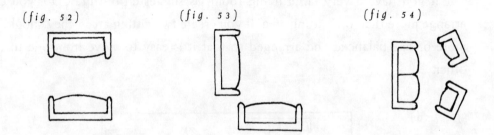

- To create a warm and friendly atmosphere, use a variety of chairs and couches that appeal to you. Commercially manufactured living room sets are monotonous and impersonal. Variety is the spice of life; it generates warmth and interest.

- If your living room has a small alcove, you can create an intimate conversation area in it. If the room doesn't have an alcove but is large enough, you can create an intimate, alcovelike conversation area by positioning a high-rise unit or cabinet and a plant in a way such as that illustrated in figure 55.

(fig. 55)

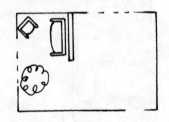

- The lighting in a romantic living room should be soft and localized. Place attractive lamps in different areas to create focal points in the room. The best places for lamps are in the sitting areas and by a special reading chair.

- If your living room has a fireplace, arrange an intimate sitting area around it. A fire is something to muse on. It can bring up the warmest feelings and thoughts between people.

- A fireplace produces heat, however, it also draws the chi out of the room. A mirror mounted over the fireplace will help counteract this effect, but it is desirable only if your fireplace is in an area that is in a positive relation to the compass direction of the room's doorway. The following guidelines will help you determine the positive and negative areas of your living room.

If your living room door faces **north**, the positive areas are the north, east, southeast, and south. The negative areas are the northeast, southwest, west, and northwest.

If your living room door faces **northeast**, the positive areas are the northeast, southwest, west, and northwest. The negative areas are the north, east, southeast, and south.

If your living room door faces **east**, the positive areas are the east, southeast, south, and north. The negative areas are the northeast, southwest, west, and northwest.

If your living room door faces **southeast**, the positive areas are the southeast, south, north, and east. The negative areas are the northeast, southwest, west, and northwest.

If your living room door faces **south**, the positive areas are the south, north, east, and southeast. The negative areas are the northeast, southwest, west, and northwest.

If your living room door faces **southwest**, the positive areas are the southwest, west, northwest, and northeast. The negative areas are the north, east, southeast, and south.

If your living room door faces **west**, the positive areas are the west, northwest, northeast, and southwest. The negative areas are the north, east, southeast, and south.

179

If your living room door faces **northwest,** the positive areas are the northwest, northeast, southwest, and west. The negative areas are the north, east, southeast, and south.

- Arrange your pictures and other decorative objects to complement your sitting areas. If you are using your living room as a combination office and living room, you can define the border between them either by hanging a row of smaller pictures in a vertical line, as illustrated in figure 56, or by creating a decorative border with stencils.

(*fig. 56*)

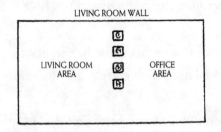

- Remember, even numbers of things heighten the romantic quality of a room. Hang pictures in pairs or in groups of even numbers. If you want to use romantically symbolic images, refer to the list of traditional symbols on page 168.
- To add a magical touch, display either Talisman 2 or Talisman 5 from the back of this book in the area of your living room that corresponds to your relationship element or element of mutual harmony. Or, display one of these talismans in the area of the marriage point.

Exercises

- If you haven't done so already, sketch a smooth line around the contours of your living room on a copy of your floor plan, as suggested by figure 48, to ascertain the flow of its chi.
- Sketch possible furniture arrangements for your sitting area that embrace the chi flow, keeping in mind the guidelines discussed in this chapter.

chapter 13

The Windows

Windows should be considered not only for their light and ventilation but for the views they hold. The following trouble spots can adversely affect your nerves in a subtle way and contribute to tensions in your relationships.

- It is not good for a window to face a road or driveway that runs directly toward or away from it, as shown for a door in figure 21 in Chapter 9.
- A window should not face a U-shaped road or overpass, called a curved blade, as shown for a door in figure 22.
- A window should not directly face the end of a cul-de-sac or T-junction, as shown for a door in figure 23.
- A window should not directly face a building situated at an angle, as shown for a door in figure 24.
- A window should not face any sharp objects pointing directly at it.
- A window should not face a dead tree or building that is falling into ruin.
- A window should not face part of another building and part of an empty lot, as shown for a door in figure 25.
- A window should not face two buildings separated by a narrow alley, as shown for a door in figure 26.
- A window should not face two buildings in which the one in back rises slightly higher than the one in front, as shown for a door in figure 27.

- A window should not face a single building that towers over all its neighbors.
- A window should not look out at water towers on top of neighboring buildings.
- A window should not face suspended electrical or telephone wires, or train tracks that are either elevated or running along the ground.
- A window should not face smokestacks.
- A window should not face a power plant, sewage plant, garbage dump, police station, firehouse, jail, hospital, funeral home, gambling hall, or anything that makes you feel uneasy.

Remedies by Compass Direction

If you detect any of these trouble spots from your windows, use the following remedies, based on the compass direction of your window. To ascertain the compass direction of a window, simply stand in front of the window with your compass and look squarely out. The direction you face is your window's compass direction.

The color remedies described here can be applied in any number of ways. You can use window treatments of an appropriate color, hang pictures beside the windows, hang stained glass in the windows, place colored objects on the windowsills, and so forth.

- If your window faces **north**, use greens or light blues in or near the window.
- If your window faces **northeast**, use whites, grays, or silver in or near the window.
- If your window faces **east**, use reds, purples, roses, or pinks in or near the window.
- If your window faces **southeast**, use reds, purples, roses, or pinks in or near the window.
- If your window faces **south**, use yellows, golds, oranges, browns, tans, or beiges in or near the window.

- If your window faces **southwest**, use whites, grays, or silver in or near the window.
- If your window faces **west**, use black or deep blues in or near the window.
- If your window faces **northwest**, use black or deep blues in or near the window.

If you don't want to employ a color remedy, use the following substitutes: where greens or light blues are indicated, use living plants or rectangular objects. Where reds, purples, roses, or pinks are indicated, use an amethyst or a triangular or pyramidal object. Where yellows, golds, oranges, browns, tans, or beiges are indicated, use crude, natural stones or square or cubic objects. Where whites, grays, or silver is indicated, use metal sculptures or round or oval objects. Where black or deep blues are indicated, use objects made of glass or crystal, including clear quartz crystals.

Light and View

It is better to have windows on two adjoining walls of a room than on one wall only. Windows on adjoining walls give much finer light and make it much easier to notice the subtle expressions on someone's face. Windows on one wall only tend to create glare. This is a common problem in apartments, especially in row houses that have windows only in the front and back.

If one or more of your rooms has windows on one wall only, you can soften the light most easily by hanging plants in the windows or by covering the windows with sheer or lace curtains. You can also recess the windows or hang a mirror, preferably a large one, on the wall adjacent to the windows' wall.

The way to recess the windows is to construct or install a wall unit (of cabinets and/or shelves) of at least 1 foot depth that completely fills the wall and frames each window. This works perfectly in a room whose window wall has two or more windows that are amply spaced. It won't work, however, on a wall of uninterrupted windows, such as those found in modern apartment buildings.

If you have a window that holds a particularly pleasant or interesting view, place an intimate sitting area around it. For instance, you can arrange a comfortable sitting area in a bay window. If you want to construct a small window seat as part of a wall unit that recesses a window, make the wall unit deep enough to contain the seat. Put a cushion on the window seat and hang attractive curtains in the window to make it more enjoyable and private.

The following vignettes will illustrate how some of the problems just delineated were remedied by my clients.

Catherine

Catherine has a one-bedroom apartment on Manhattan's Upper East Side. Before consulting with me, she felt anxious and lonely. Outside her windows, all of which face the same direction, are a number of objects like water towers, smokestacks, and barbed wire. Upon taking a compass reading I found that her windows face the southeast. Because reds, purples, roses, and pinks are appropriate remedies for trouble spots seen from a southeast-facing window, Catherine chose to put rose-colored venetian blinds in her bedroom window and a purple-and-rose stained-glass decoration, in addition to red and pink flowers, in the living room window. Soon after she had implemented these and other feng shui remedies, she began to enjoy herself a lot more and eventually formed a new and happy relationship.

Harry and Louise

Harry and Louise live in an apartment whose kitchen and dining room windows overlook a hospital. Because they didn't like the dining room, it had become little more than a storage area. In other words, it was a mess, and it only made them feel uncomfortable and discontented. When I took a compass reading I found that the dining room windows face south. Because yellows, golds, oranges, browns, tans, and beiges were the appropriate colors to use as remedies, Louise and Harry agreed to hang warm yellow curtains and blond-wood venetian blinds at the windows, and to paint the dining room walls yellow. After they had taken out all the clutter and decorated the room, their feelings about it changed for the better. As a result, they began entertaining their friends at home more and began enjoying each other a lot more as well.

Exercise

Look out your windows to check the view for any of the trouble spots listed in this chapter. Note on your floor plan and/or Things to Do list any trouble spots you find. Next take a compass reading of your window's direction by standing squarely in front of it, looking out. If you have any doubt about the exact compass direction you are facing, refer to figure 4 on page 132. Once you have determined your window's compass direction, review the remedies just discussed and make a note of your solution on your floor plan and/or in your Things to Do list.

For example, suppose you can see suspended electrical wires outside your living room window and find that the window faces west. In your Things to Do list you would write, "Trouble spot outside the west-facing living room window." Then choose a possible remedy and write it down, for example, "Put clear quartz crystal on the living room windowsill." Repeat this process for all your windows. However, wait until you have read all of Part Two before you begin implementing your solutions. You will find extensive instructions on the use of colors in Chapter 15.

special problems
and solutions

Houses and apartments often have problematic designs that make the people who live in them feel uncomfortable without knowing why. Design
problems also affect the quality of people's relationships, making it difficult to
promote or nurture love affairs. Examine the layout of your home in light of the
material in this chapter, and note any remedies you might need to utilize.

Doorways

The doorways inside your home determine its patterns of movement. When doors
are positioned correctly, the movement from room to room is smooth and easy, but
when doors are awkwardly positioned, movement is awkward and space is wasted.

- Doors that are near the corners of rooms are the most efficient because they
  allow for maximum use of space. Doors in the middle of a wall, as shown in
  figure 57, split the room in half. Unless the room is very large, or is a dining room in which you would place the table squarely in the middle, such
  doorways interfere with the function of the room. If you have a room whose
  door is in the middle of a wall, hang drapes at the doorframe to give a
  greater feeling of containment. If the room is long and narrow, however,
  arrange it in two parts, as suggested in figure 58, using the doorway to mark
  their boundaries.

(fig. 57)   (fig. 58)

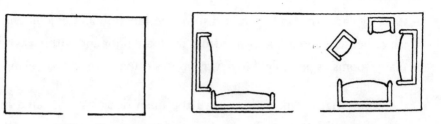

- Rooms with two or more doors invite through traffic. If the doors are aligned to one side of the room, as illustrated in figure 59, this is not a big problem. However, if the doors are aligned such as those suggested in figures 60 and 61, the line of traffic will interfere with the room's function and render part of the room more or less useless.

(fig. 59)   (fig. 60)

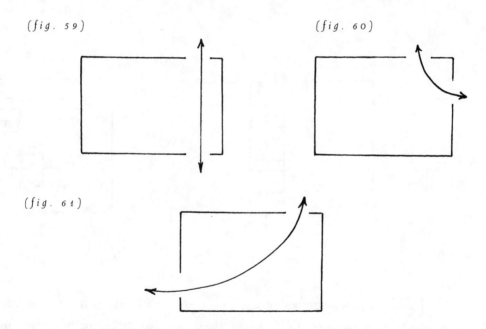

(fig. 61)

If you have a room with two doors as illustrated in figures 59 and 60, place bookcases or hang pictures in the smaller area defined by the line of traffic. If you have a room with two doors like that illustrated in figure 61, either close off one of the doors or arrange the furniture to control the line of traffic and expand the use of the room. If the room is very large, create two sitting areas in relation to the two doors.

Stairways

A stairway can either enhance or disrupt the function and enjoyment of a home. Ideally, the stairs should be visible from the main door and within easy access from as many rooms as possible. However, houses often have the following problems.

- Stairs that run directly toward the main door, as illustrated in figure 62, cause the chi to run out the door and presage losses of money. If your home has this problem, either reconstruct the staircase to resemble figure 63, or place an attractively framed mirror on the door wall beside or even above the door to reflect the stairs. A small mirror will do. You can also place a live standing plant by the foot of the staircase, providing there is enough light and space in the entrance hall to accommodate it.

(fig. 62)　　　　　　　　　　(fig. 63)

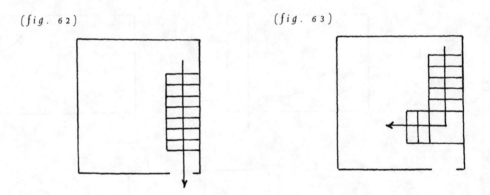

- Tightly winding spiral staircases, especially without risers, are hazardous. Aside from their obvious danger, they can also subliminally attract untoward conditions into your life. An obviously bad place for you to have such a staircase is at the marriage point or compass area in your home that corresponds to your relationship element or element of mutual harmony. If your home has this problem, put live potted plants under the stairs to absorb the negative chi, and keep the stairway well lit.

Hallways

Hallways are like roads. They link the functions of the different areas of your home. However, houses and apartments often have the following hallway problems.

- A hallway that is long and narrow causes the chi to rush through like an arrow. If you have such a problematic hallway, place two, four, six, or eight full-length mirrors, spaced at regular intervals, along one of its walls to divert the chi.
- A door other than the main door at the end of a long, narrow hall, as illustrated in figure 64, receives the arrowlike current of chi generated by the hallway. If your home has this problem, place a full-length mirror on the side of the door that faces into the hallway to deflect the chi.

(fig. 64)

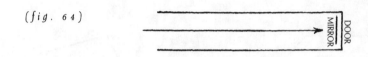

- A hallway with doors directly opposite each other, as illustrated in figure 65, creates a tense atmosphere. If you have a hallway with this problem, hang some mirrors or interesting and beautiful pictures on the walls beside the doors to divert attention.

(fig. 65)

- A hallway with doors crowded on one end, as illustrated in figure 66, causes irritability. If your home has this problem, hang soothing pictures or use soothing colors in the hallway.

(fig. 66)

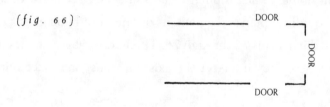

Irregular Shapes

The best and simplest shapes for the layout of a home or room are the rectangle and the square. Irregular shapes, such as the L-shape (figure 67), the dustpan shape (figure 68), trapezoids (figure 69), trapeziums (figure 70), or shapes with many angles (figure 71), cause a variety of problems. The L-shape, dustpan shape, and shapes with many angles can complicate the flow of chi in your home and your activities, while trapezoids and trapeziums can confuse your sense of purpose.

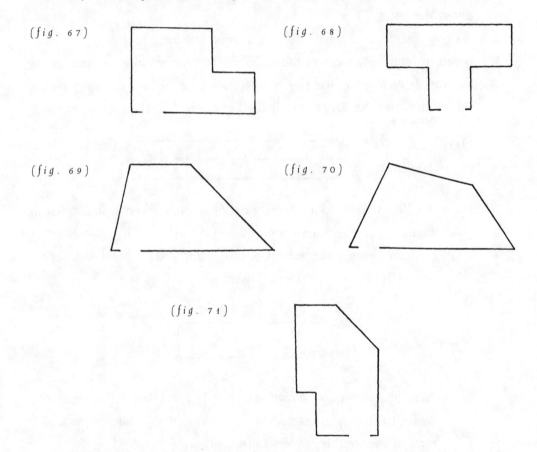

(fig. 67)

(fig. 68)

(fig. 69)

(fig. 70)

(fig. 71)

If the shape of your home, or any room in your home, resembles any of these shapes, take a copy of your floor plan and extend its outlines until you get a square or rectangle, as illustrated in figures 72 through 76. Then draw diagonal lines from corner to corner, note where they intersect the existing walls, and place mirrors at those points.

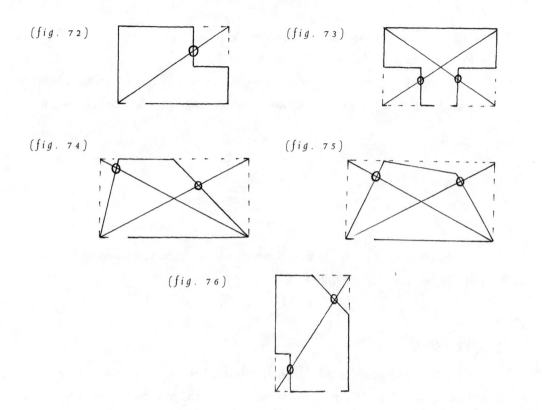

(fig. 72)   *(fig. 73)*   *(fig. 74)*   *(fig. 75)*   *(fig. 76)*

As an alternative to this method, you can mirror entire walls, as illustrated in figures 77 and 78.

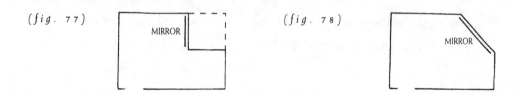

(fig. 77)   *(fig. 78)*

MIRROR   MIRROR

The mirror in figure 77 creates the illusion of opening the space and filling in the missing area, as indicated by the dotted lines. The mirror in figure 78, placed on the slanted wall, creates the illusion of symmetry in an otherwise asymmetrical room.

Here are the basic rules for mirroring entire walls as remedies for irregularly shaped spaces:

- Place mirrors on the walls backing the "missing areas" (see figure 77).
- Place mirrors on slanted walls (see figure 78).
- Avoid placing mirrors too close to and squarely facing a doorway, as illustrated in figure 79, unless you want to discourage people from coming in.

(fig. 79)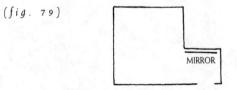

In addition to mirrors, irregularly shaped spaces can be remedied with colors. We will discuss this method fully in Chapter 15.

Exercises

- Check your home for any problems related to its doorways, stairway, or hallways as described in this chapter. If you find any problems, make note of them, along with their remedies, on your floor plan and/or Things to Do list.
- If your home, or a room in your home, has an irregular shape, decide whether you want to remedy it with mirrors. If you do, choose which of the two methods discussed in this chapter you intend to use, and make a note of it on your floor plan and/or Things to Do list.

color schemes

Color is one of the most versatile and powerful aspects of feng shui. When used correctly, not only does it create the effect of balance and harmony in your home but it encourages warmth and love between people. There are different levels to the application of color. Let's look at each of them, and see how they fit together.

Yin and Yang Hues

Except for white, which is yang, and black, which is yin, every color has both yin and yang hues. Yin hues are the cooler, darker, or more subdued shades of a color, while yang hues are the warmer and brighter shades.

As a general rule, try to keep the yin and yang hues in balance throughout your home, giving more emphasis to yang hues in the more common areas and yin hues in the more private areas. For example, use warm colors more in the dining area and living room than in the bedroom. Conversely, use subdued or deeper colors more in the bedroom than in the dining area and living room. In other words, do not use too much of a somber color in your dining area or living room, or too much of a vibrant color in your bedroom.

Your Personal Colors

Include the color that corresponds to your personal element, relationship element, or element of mutual harmony in the general scheme of your home. You can do this by selecting carpets, drapery, or furniture upholstery with your colors; or by painting the walls.

Remember, if your personal element, relationship element, or element of mutual harmony is Water, use black or deep blues with white. A room done entirely in white and black resonates to the element Water.

If your personal element, relationship element, or element of mutual harmony is Wood, use any of the hues of green, teal, turquoise, or the lighter hues of blue.

If your personal element, relationship element, or element of mutual harmony is Fire, use any of the hues of red, purple, violet, lavender, rose, and pink.

If your personal element, relationship element, or element of mutual harmony is Earth, use any of the hues of yellow, gold, orange, brown, tan, and beige.

If your personal element, relationship element, or element of mutual harmony is Metal, use any of the hues of white, gray, and silver.

Using Colors to Balance Protruding and Indented Areas

The following method should be applied only where you find a protruding or indented area in the floor plan of your home as a whole, not for a single room. A protruding area, as illustrated in figure 80, juts out of the main body of the space. Conversely, an indented area, as illustrated in figure 81, looks as though it were missing.

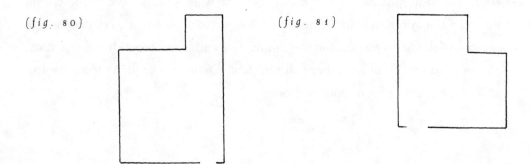

(fig. 80)   *(fig. 81)*

While protruding and indented shapes appear similar to some of the irregular shapes discussed in Chapter 14, they are different. For an area to be defined as protruding or indented, it should involve no more than one-third the length or width of the main body of the space, as shown by figures 82 and 83. If you don't want to deal with this much precision, however, you may define a protruding or indented area as involving noticeably less than half the length or width of the main body of the space.

(fig. 82) *(fig. 83)*

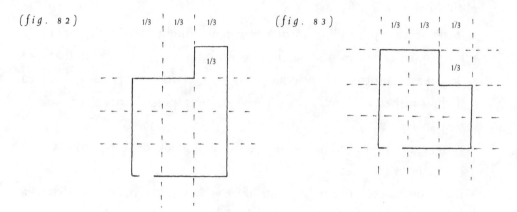

Because we can judge protruded and indented areas by their compass directions and corresponding elements, we can remedy the chi imbalances they generate by applying appropriate colors. To use this method, take a copy of your floor plan, extend its outlines to form a square or rectangle, and determine its central compass point and compass directions as you learned to do in How to Use Part Two. Figure 84 shows a southeast area that is indented and a northwest area that is protruding.

(fig. 84)

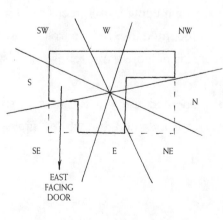

Let's look at the color remedies for various protruding and indented areas of your home. In applying these remedies, you don't have to paint entire rooms or areas unless, of course, you want to. You can introduce a recommended color in the form of a picture, a piece of furniture, and so on. The right color, in however large or small a form, acts like an acupuncture needle; it stimulates the chi flow of the treated area to resolve its imbalance.

Protruding Areas

- If the **north** is protruding, introduce greens or light blues in that area.
- If the **northeast** is protruding, introduce whites, grays, or silver in that area.
- If the **east** is protruding, introduce reds, purples, roses, or pinks in that area.
- If the **southeast** is protruding, introduce reds, purples, roses, or pinks in that area.
- If the **south** is protruding, introduce yellows, golds, oranges, browns, tans, or beiges in that area.
- If the **southwest** is protruding, introduce whites, grays, or silver in that area.
- If the **west** is protruding, introduce black or deep blues in that area.
- If the **northwest** is protruding, introduce black or deep blues in that area.

Indented Areas

- If the **north** area is indented, use black or deep blues around it.
- If the **northeast** area is indented, use yellows, golds, oranges, browns, tans, or beiges around it.
- If the **east** area is indented, use greens or light blues around it.
- If the **southeast** area is indented, use greens or light blues around it.
- If the **south** area is indented, use reds, purples, roses, or pinks around it.
- If the **southwest** area is indented, use yellows, golds, oranges, browns, tans, or beiges around it.
- If the **west** area is indented, use whites, grays, or silver around it.
- If the **northwest** area is indented, use whites, grays, or silver around it.

Balancing All Areas with the Element of Your Main Door

While the element that corresponds to the compass direction of your main door rules your entire home (Water for north, Wood for east, and so on), each of the eight compass areas inside your home has its own corresponding element. Because each of the elements has harmonious and discordant relations with the other elements, certain areas in your home are in a more harmonious relation to the element of your main door than others. By applying special colors to those areas in your home that are out of harmony with the element of the main door, you can transform their chi and bring your whole home into harmony and balance.

As with the preceding material, you will need to work with your floor plan to apply this method. Take a fresh copy of your floor plan, and extend its outlines to form a square or rectangle if needed. Then mark its central point, its main door's compass direction, and its eight compass areas. Based on the compass direction of your main door, you can balance your home as follows:

- If your main door faces **north,** use whites, grays, or silver in the northeast and southwest areas, and greens or light blues with a touch of black or deep blues in the west and northwest areas, as illustrated in figure 85.
- If your main door faces **northeast,** use reds, purples, roses, or pinks in the east and southeast areas, and whites, grays, or silver in the north and south areas, with an additional touch of an earth tone (yellow, gold, orange, brown, and so on) in the south area, as illustrated in figure 86.
- If your main door faces **east,** use reds, purples, roses, or pinks in the southwest and northeast areas, and black or deep blues in the west and northwest areas, as illustrated in figure 87.
- If your main door faces **southeast,** use reds, purples, roses, or pinks in the southwest and northeast areas, and black or deep blues in the west and northwest areas, as illustrated in figure 88.
- If your main door faces **south,** use whites, grays, or silver in the southwest and northeast areas, and earth tones (yellow, gold, orange, brown, and so on) in the west and northwest areas, as illustrated in figure 89.

197

- If your main door faces **southwest,** use reds, purples, roses, or pinks in the east and southeast areas, and whites, grays, or silver in the north and south areas, with a touch of an earth tone (yellow, gold, orange, brown, and so on) in the south area, as illustrated in figure 90.

- If your main door faces **west,** use greens or light blues with a touch of black or deep blues in the north area, black or deep blues in the east and southeast areas, and earth tones (yellow, gold, orange, brown, and so on) in the south area, as shown in figure 91.

- If your main door faces **northwest,** use greens or light blues with a touch of black or deep blues in the north area, black or deep blues in the east and southeast areas, and earth tones (yellow, gold, orange, brown, and so on) in the south area, as illustrated in figure 92.

(fig. 85)

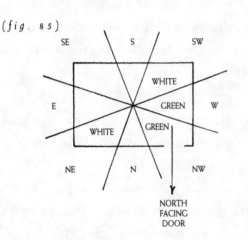

(fig. 86)

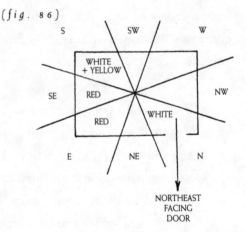

(fig. 87)

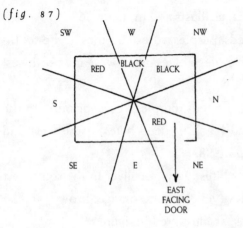

(fig. 88)

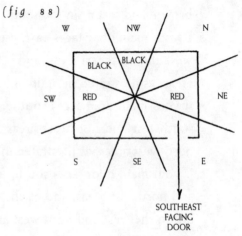

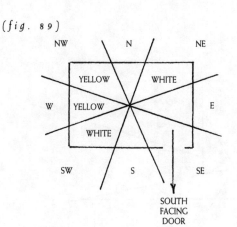

(fig. 89)

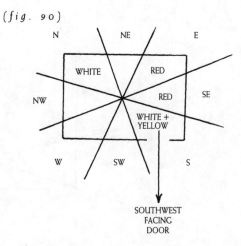

(fig. 90)

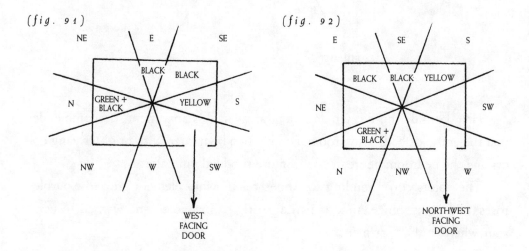

(fig. 91) (fig. 92)

   The following vignettes combine all these guidelines, and demonstrate how I have used colors to help my clients improve their love lives.

Anne

Anne was discontented with her personal life. She had been dating two men but because neither of them was compatible had no intention of making a serious commitment. She was hoping for the right man to come along and was anxious. Anne's personal element is Metal, and her relationship element is Fire. She lives in an apartment whose floor plan is illustrated in figure 93.

(*fig. 9 3*)

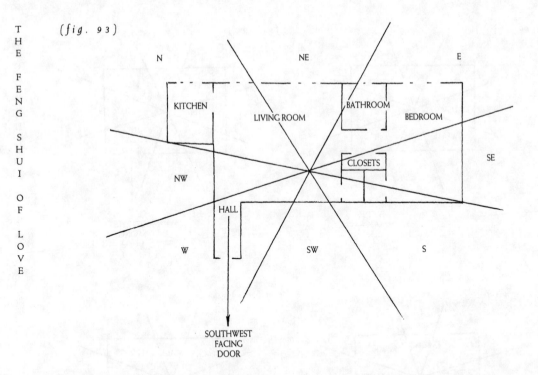

First, considering the yin and yang areas in this apartment, I recommended that the entrance hall, living room, and kitchen be treated with brighter yang colors and the bedroom be treated with more subdued yin colors.

The colors corresponding to Anne's relationship element are reds, purples, roses, and pinks. Since Anne is partial to the color violet, she wanted to use it somewhere in the apartment.

There are two protruding areas in Anne's apartment: the kitchen, which is in the north, and the entrance hall, to the west. Because green or light blue is the appropriate color for a protruding north area, Anne decided to put café curtains that are light green, a yang hue, in the kitchen window. She also decided to hang a group of romantic black-and-white photos in the entrance hall, since black is the appropriate color remedy for a protruding west area.

Because the door to Anne's apartment faces southwest, the areas to the north and south need whites, grays, or silver, and the areas to the east and southeast need reds, purples, roses, or pinks. Anne chose to paint the kitchen, which is in the north area, white. She then chose to paint the bedroom a pale violet and to hang two small pictures in silver frames on the wall in the south area of that room. She also decided to paint the bathroom rose, to put rose venetian blinds on the bathroom and bedroom windows, and to hang plum-colored curtains on the bedroom windows as well. Because Anne's personal element is Metal, she then chose to decorate her living room entirely in tones of white, gray, and silver.

After she had reorganized and painted her apartment, Anne's interest in meeting new people was refreshed. Before long she was introduced to someone she found really attractive. A new and fortunate love relationship began that eventually led to marriage.

George and Lucy

George and Lucy are a married couple whose element of mutual harmony is Earth. They called me in to look at an apartment they had just bought. The floor plan of this apartment is illustrated in figure 94.

(fig. 9 4)

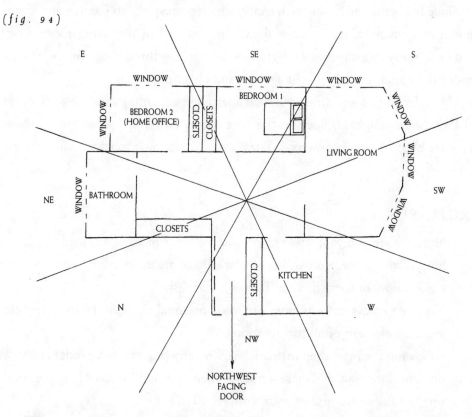

There are three indented areas in the layout: to the west, to the north, and to the east.

201

Instead of using a color remedy for the indented north area, George and Lucy placed a series of full-length mirrors on the north wall of the entrance hall. Because white was needed to remedy the indented west area, they chose to paint the kitchen and living room walls entirely white. They also chose to use deep green window treatments in the bathroom and in bedroom 2 to remedy the indented east area.

Because the door of the apartment faces northwest, the areas to the east and southeast need some black or deep blue; the area to the south needs yellows, golds, oranges, browns, tans, or beiges; and the area to the north needs some green with black or deep blues. Lucy and George, therefore, chose to put kilims that have some black in them on the floors of both bedrooms. They also chose to hang beige curtains and put a rug with various earth tones in the living room, and to hang a small picture with predominant green and black on the side of the closet in the north area.

Since the beige and other earth tones, which correspond to George and Lucy's element of mutual harmony, were already introduced in the living room, Lucy decided to use various beiges and yellows with white throughout the remaining areas of their apartment to give it a warm and cheerful feeling.

Upon decorating and arranging their apartment according to this plan, George and Lucy were delighted. Because they are happy living and entertaining there, they have become very prosperous. They are now planning to start a family.

Exercises

- Note the yin and yang areas of your home for choices of subdued or vibrant hues of the colors you will use. Mark these areas on your floor plan and make a note of them in your Things to Do list.

- Note the colors corresponding to your personal element, relationship element, or element of mutual harmony.

- Following the preceding instructions, find any protruding or indented areas on your floor plan, and make a note of their appropriate color remedies both on your floor plan and in your Things to Do list.

- Ascertain the appropriate colors to balance the compass areas of your home with the element of its main door. Make notes of these color remedies in their appropriate places on your floor plan as well as in your Things to Do list.

- In the areas that don't need special color remedies, you can freely apply the colors that correspond to your personal element, relationship element, or element of mutual harmony. Even in those areas that need special color remedies, you can apply the colors that correspond to your personal element and so on. However, be careful to avoid color clashes.

- Once you have all your colors outlined, decide how you are going to apply them: by painting the walls, hanging pictures, using carpets or furniture? Use your imagination. Write down your ideas in your Things to Do list.

Remedies for Areas of Concern in Your Love Relationship

○ Special problems have special solutions. In addition to all that you have gathered so far, the following procedures will focus the chi of your home to help you overcome whatever obstacles stand in the way of your happiness in love. If any of the concerns addressed here are yours, include their remedies in your Things to Do list.

The remedies here require the use of your compass. You can implement them either from the compass orientation of the main door of your home or from the compass orientation of the door of a specific room, such as your bedroom. Remember, the correct way to judge the compass orientation of any door is by looking out.

If You Seek a Relationship

Creating a special love altar is an excellent thing to do if you do not have a relationship but desire one. It can be arranged on a small table, a nightstand, a bureau, or a shelf attached to the wall.

Place personally meaningful objects on your love altar. You can include a romantic picture, some mementos, a love poem, beautiful crystals, candles, a vase of flowers (two roses would be perfect), and whatever else you associate with your wishes for love. If you have a personal love charm, such as a ring or other piece of jewelry suggested on page 42, keep it on your altar when you are not wearing it.

You may also cut out Talisman 5 from the back of this book, mount it on a mat whose color corresponds to your relationship element, and place it on your altar, hang it on the wall above your altar, or just hang it on the wall by itself if the idea of creating an altar doesn't appeal to you.

Put your love altar or talisman in the area of your home or room that is called Generating Chi. The way to locate this special area is as follows:

- If the door faces **north**, the area of Generating Chi is in the southeast.
- If the door faces **northeast**, the area of Generating Chi is in the southwest.
- If the door faces **east**, the area of Generating Chi is in the south.
- If the door faces **southeast**, the area of Generating Chi is in the north.
- If the door faces **south**, the area of Generating Chi is in the east.
- If the door faces **southwest**, the area of Generating Chi is in the northeast.
- If the door faces **west**, the area of Generating Chi is in the northwest.
- If the door faces **northwest**, the area of Generating Chi is in the west.

If Your Relationship Is Troubled

You can also create a special love altar if your relationship is troubled and you wish to make it better. However, hanging a talisman on the wall is all you really need to do. Cut out Talisman 5 from the back of this book, mount it on a mat whose color corresponds to your element of mutual harmony, and hang it on a wall in the area of your home or room called the Heavenly Healer. The way to locate this powerful area is as follows:

- If the door faces **north**, the area of the Heavenly Healer is in the east.
- If the door faces **northeast**, the area of the Heavenly Healer is in the north-west.
- If the door faces **east**, the area of the Heavenly Healer is in the north.
- If the door faces **southeast**, the area of the Heavenly Healer is in the south.

- If the door faces **south**, the area of the Heavenly Healer is in the southeast.
- If the door faces **southwest**, the area of the Heavenly Healer is in the west.
- If the door faces **west**, the area of the Heavenly Healer is in the southwest.
- If the door faces **northwest**, the area of the Heavenly Healer is in the northeast.

If You Wish to Nurture Your Relationship

Creating a special love altar or hanging Talisman 5 from the back of this book on the wall are both good ways to nurture your relationship. However, you may prefer to use a romantic photo of you and your partner. Mount the photo on a mat whose color corresponds to your element of mutual harmony, and hang it in the area of your home or room called Longevity. The way to locate this special area is as follows:

- If the door faces **north**, the area of Longevity is in the south.
- If the door faces **northeast**, the area of Longevity is in the west.
- If the door faces **east**, the area of Longevity is in the southeast.
- If the door faces **southeast**, the area of Longevity is in the east.
- If the door faces **south**, the area of Longevity is in the north.
- If the door faces **southwest**, the area of Longevity is in the northwest.
- If the door faces **west**, the area of Longevity is in the northeast.
- If the door faces **northwest**, the area of Longevity is in the southwest.

chapter 17

House Blessing

We have now come full circle. In Chapter 1 we discussed the way your inner mental state affects your environment. In this chapter I would like to give you a simple, effective technique for simultaneously clearing your home of negativity and imbuing it with positive, loving chi.

The entire universe is pervaded by chi. Every place, therefore, is a convergence point of chi. Not only does chi radiate from the core essence of your being like a star but it comes to you through the air you breathe, the water you drink, and the food you eat. It comes to you from heaven and earth, the sun, the moon, the planets and stars, the eight compass directions, and the five elements.

Chi is both yin and yang. It is yin in the earth and yang in the heavens. It is yin in the north and west, and yang in the south and east. In your body, it is yin on your left side and yang on your right side if you are right-handed, or yang on your left side and yin on your right side if you are left-handed.

In nature the forces of yin and yang are always in dynamic balance. Their harmonious interaction produces all things. When the forces of yin and yang in your body, emotions, mind, and environment are brought into balance and harmony, your life and relationships can't help but flourish. When the forces of yin and yang in your life and environment become unbalanced, the quality of your life and relationships disintegrates.

Because there is nothing that is not subject to impermanence, the keys for keeping a harmonious and balanced way of life are acceptance, adaptation, and adjustment. If you accept and are able to adapt and adjust to changes while maintaining a loving and compassionate view, your environment and relationships will always remain healthy and secure.

The technique for imbuing your home with positive, loving chi is as follows. Sit comfortably on a firm chair in a quiet area of your home. Sit with your hips close to the edge of the seat. Sit up straight, looking neither up nor down but directly forward. Relax your shoulders, and rest your hands, palms on your thighs, as close to your knees as is comfortable. Do not lean forward or to either side.

Lightly close your eyes. Breathe naturally and calmly. Smile gently to expand your third eye. Smile deep down in your heart. When you smile from your heart, breathe naturally, and are relaxed and at attention, you will become open and able to receive cosmic chi.

Breathe in the chi from above, below, and around you all at the same time. Breathe in the chi not only through your nose but through all the pores of your body. As you breathe in focus the chi at your heart, and as you breathe out let the chi radiate from your heart. Breathe light and love from the core of your being, and let it permeate your entire home. Do this for as long as it feels comfortable. When you feel complete simply release yourself by dedicating the benefits of this practice to the joy and contentment of all sentient beings in the universe. You can repeat this simple practice as often as you wish.

I wish you great good fortune and happiness in using this book. If you want to consult with me or contact me, you can either write to me or visit my Web site. My mailing address is T. Raphael Simons, 545 Eighth Avenue, Suite 401, New York, New York 10018. My Web site address is www.TRS-fengshui.com.

The Talismans

The talismans that follow were painted by world-renowned calligrapher, painter, and seal engraver Zeng Xianwen, a fellow of the Chinese Academy of the Arts and a member of many other calligraphers associations.

Born into a noble and ancient family of scholars in Jinzhou in southern Liaoning and now residing in the United States, Zeng Xianwen has had his works featured in numerous publications and art exhibitions in China and is becoming well known in the United States. His works are in the collections of several museums in China. He has been called an Art Talent Treasure by the Chinese government.

1. INSIGHTFUL ACTIVITY

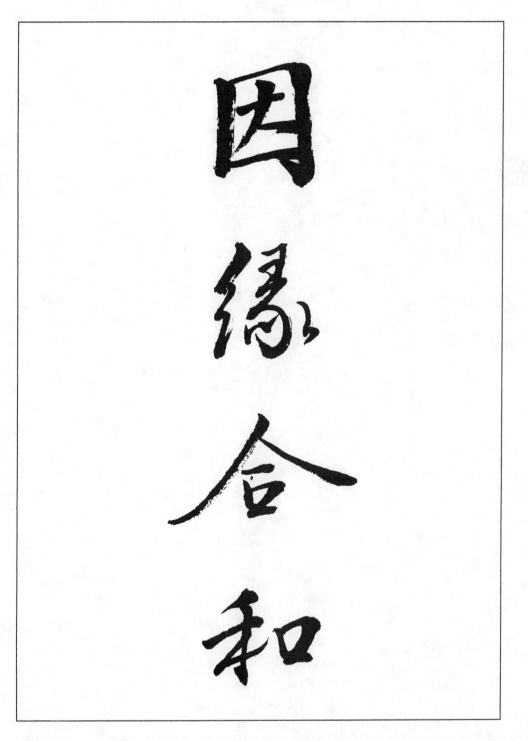

2. THE INTERACTIONS OF THE NATURAL FORCES PRODUCE
THE HARMONY OF THE UNIVERSE

3. SUCCESS

4. PROTECTION

5. LOVE

Index